Building Financial
Decision-Making
Models

Building Financial Decision-Making Models

An Introduction to Principles and Procedures

Donald R. Moscato

A Division of American Management Associations

Library of Congress Cataloging in Publication Data

Moscato, Donald R
  Building financial decision-making models.

  Bibliography: p. 129
  Includes index.
  1. Corporations—Finance—Mathematical models.
  I. Title.
  HG4011.M5673   658.1'5'0724   80-65704
  ISBN 0-8144-5609-X

First Printing

To Aurora, Lori, and Eric

Preface

TEN years ago a book of this kind would not have been written. Sure, there were organizations engaged in financial modeling, but for the most part, the area was left to a specialized group of technical types who were little understood or valued by management. Today, most large and medium-size organizations are involved with or thinking about the pros and cons of financial modeling.

This book is written for the manager and not the specialist. Its purpose is to help the manager get started with financial modeling. Within a few short pages no writer can purport to communicate all the technical details and considerations of a topic as widely perceived as financial modeling, but I have set out to achieve the following objectives:

1. Describe in nontechnical terms what financial modeling is.
2. Discuss the various types of financial models and their distinguishing characteristics.
3. Clarify the numerous organizational support issues and their political ramifications.

4. Enumerate a step-by-step process for starting a financial modeling effort in your organization.
5. Establish the necessary linkage with the firm's information system.
6. Elaborate on where models can go wrong and what can help them go right.

Now that you know what the book is trying to achieve, let us spend a few moments in establishing what the book is *not*. It is not a text in operations research/management or decision sciences. It is not an "all-you-need-to-know" book. Finally, it is not a one-sided sales pitch that presents modeling as a panacea for your company's planning or control problems.

Throughout the pages of this book you will read about some of the most successfully used and promising approaches to the modeling of financial situations to aid in the decision support process. Many techniques of modeling have been omitted by choice because in the author's opinion they are not as widespread, potentially useful, or relevant as those included. Perhaps in time the balance may change from one approach or technique to another. Time alone will tell.

Donald R. Moscato

Contents

1

Financial Modeling— What It Is

A model can be defined as a representation or abstraction of reality. A mathematical model is a symbolic representation of reality. A mathematical financial model, therefore, is a symbolic representation of the financial aspects of an organization. According to our definition, both a balance sheet and a profit-and-loss statement are financial models. The same can be said for an organization's budget. All these examples are symbolic representations of financial characteristics of the firm.

By this time the reader is probably thinking that a financial model is something more complex, depicting a very large number of factors related by a series of equations that can be analyzed or solved only by means of a modern high-speed computer with extensive storage capacity. Let us pause for a moment and see whether this is true. A mathematical model contains a set of variables which represent key factors involved in the phenomenon that is to be modeled. Are not the quantities sales, gross margin, depreciation, cost of goods sold, and so on examples of factors affecting the financial side of a business? Next, a model has structure—that is, it defines certain relationships among the factors. In the case of our three simple examples—the balance sheet, the profit-and-loss statement, and the budget—the basic structures are defined by addition and subtraction of accounts, typically in accordance with generally accepted accounting principles. The simplicity of their structures does not disqualify our examples as financial models.

Classifying Financial Models

If complexity is not a defining characteristic of financial models, how is a manager expected to distinguish the various types of financial models available to an organization? There are many different ways to classify financial models. In this book we will examine four distinguishing characteristics: time horizon, nature of variables, solution methodology, and functional objective.

Time Horizon

The time horizon for a financial model is one of the most critical parameters the manager or user of the model has to define. Some decisions are of a much shorter time span than others and require an approach to the modeling effort that is significantly different from those appropriate for longer-term decisions. For purposes of this book we will define three distinct time horizons and corresponding models: long-term planning models, near-term control-type models, and short-term operational or transactional models. Obviously, the exact time specified for each horizon varies depending on the type of industry the firm is in. For example, long term for a forest-products firm is quite different from what it is for a toy manufacturing operation. We shall show at a later time that setting the time horizon for the financial model has a direct impact on data requirements, source of model information, and parameter forecasting requirements.

The choice of the time horizon is directly related to the type of decision support system that is needed. If, for example, you are interested in managing the daily balances in bank accounts or the daily inventory levels of a department store, your needs are clearly for a short-term model requiring transactional-type data directly from the organization's data base in a highly disaggregated form. Monitoring at a detailed level places extensive demands on the firm's data processing resources. It is possible to have an excellent short-term model, proved to be accurate, only to realize that there is an ineffective data gathering and reporting system in place to support the model with timely, accurate data. This point should not be underestimated in designing short-term financial models for organizations or departments that have a known history of poor data processing support.

Long-term models are typically of the planning type and have as their function the support of the strategic planning effort. These models are concerned less with detail or transactional data than with data on trends or opportunities. General economic data on the firm's markets, whether they be national or international in scope, are usually required. These external data can come from many sources and are readily available from commercial services. This does not preclude the organization from collecting and maintaining its own external data, but most of the firms using planning models make use of the services of outside data bases in combination with their own internal business data files.

It should be noted that planning models often must rely on data of a much "softer" nature than do shorter-term models. This is because of the "fuzziness" of some of the key variables (such as the environment) appearing in planning models.

Although models can be used effectively to support the

planning function, no model, however sophisticated, should be used to actually "do" planning, that is, to derive a plan in a mechanical way without the contribution of human judgment.

Nature of Variables

In developing any financial model the question of coping with the uncertainty of the values for the variables must surface. The manner in which this question is answered leads to our second distinction: deterministic versus probabilistic financial models.

The reader is aware of the uncertain nature of financial decision making. Virtually all factors are variable, at least in the long run. However, the model builder can assume that the values of all variables within the model are known with certainty. This type of model is referred to as a deterministic model. For example, in developing a budgeting model, the decision maker assumes that all the variables and relationships are known and remain fixed in value during the running of the model. The key word is *assumes*. The model user, as well as the model developer (they can be the same person), must realize the implications of this key assumption underlying all deterministic models. How he copes with the uncertainty of the model's values will be treated in later chapters on sensitivity analysis. Suffice it to say that the successful model builder should never ignore the effects of uncertainty on the outcomes predicted by the model. At the present time, perhaps the most widely used type of financial modeling is deterministic simulation. This type of model will be described later in the book.

If one or more of the factors in a financial model are allowed to vary, then we have a probabilistic model. The more variables are described probabilistically, the more complex the model is. One of the most perplexing aspects of dealing with a probabilistic financial model is obtaining the estimates for the variables under consideration. Managers often find this task so cumbersome that they choose to trade off model realism with model simplicity and revert to a deterministic formulation. The compromise position, and the one which I adhere to religiously, is to treat only those variables as probabilistic that must be treated in this fashion. Often a variable which was treated as necessarily random could be treated as deterministic with no adverse effects on the outcome of the modeling effort. Once again, we refer the reader to the chapter on sensitivity analysis for further discussion on this topic.

Solution Methodology

This classification of financial models is somewhat technical. Nevertheless, managers should be aware of the distinction, because it can have a profound effect on the way in which they will use the model. At least two types of models can be distinguished under the heading of solution methodology: optimization models and simulation procedures.

In the context of financial modeling, optimization means determining the best way to achieve an objective with the limited resources that are available. Given a statement of objective such as "maximize profit" or "minimize cost" and a related set of constraints such as a limited budget or working capital restrictions, the model is solved for the optimum solution. The discerning reader will note that the optimum solution to the model is not necessarily the best solution to the real-world opportunity. This statement is based on the definition of a model as a representation of reality. A model must be evaluated by the decision maker as an integral element in the decision-making process. A gap will always exist between model results and reality. The technical term for a procedure deriving an optimum solution is an algorithm. It should be pointed out that there are many financial decisions that, at the present time, cannot be modeled effectively using optimization procedures. However, in situations where they do exist, optimization algorithms have proved to be of benefit.

What is the manager to do if the nature of the application to be modeled is not amenable to optimization procedures? Other types of solution methodologies exist to handle such applications. The principal one that will be discussed in this book is simulation. With simulation there does not exist an optimum solution. Rather, a model is formulated and applied under different conditions to observe the results on the designated measure of effectiveness such as ROI, profits, or market share. No one "best" solution is generated. What results is a sample of possible solutions given the mix of input values for the variables. The manager uses the resulting outcomes as a base for further experimentation or model reformulation or, if he is satisfied with the analysis, for a decision. More will be said of simulation in a later chapter.

Functional Objective

The last classification scheme for financial models that will be discussed has to do with its functional objective. The purpose of our model might be to generate a forecast, in which case we have a financial forecasting model. Most planning and control models assume the existence of a forecast. Often the financial manager is intimately involved in the generation and testing of forecasting models. More will be said of this approach in a later chapter.

In many instances the objective of modeling is to explore many different scenarios that depict slight changes from a base case. Often the base case is modeled or described in mathematical terms, and perturbations are introduced. For most studies of this type, the current situation is used as the base case. Financial managers are able to experiment on the model by introducing their views of the key input factors and observing the effects on the output measures under review. The best-known example of this approach is simulation combined with sensitivity analysis. Management may also incorporate key input factors into its model and attempt to solve the given relationships in such a way that a clear course of action is indicated, showing what ought to be done to achieve the results depicted in the model. This approach typically requires an optimization-type model. Regardless of how we choose to classify financial models, one thing is absolutely certain. A model is but a representation of reality; there will always be a gap between the output of the model and the decision to be made. We can refer to this as the judgment gap. The better the manager understands the strengths and limitations of the model, the better he can close that judgment gap and make the best possible decision. We can never eliminate uncertainty, but through modeling we can better understand what the future impact of various strategies will be.

I have frequently used an analogy to try to convey the idea that modeling is a process and not just the creation of a product—in this case, a model. We have all around us vehicles to extend our limited capabilities—for example, power steering in automobiles, hydraulic lifts, and so on. We should use the process of modeling—that is, data gathering, formulation, testing, and so forth—as a vehicle to learn more about the system being modeled. Just as exercising the muscles in our body enables us to learn more about our limits and capabilities, so should the process of modeling enable us to learn more about the dynamics of the variables under review.

The knowledge obtained from the process of modeling will prove to be invaluable in the closing of the judgmental gap. Whether we get personally involved in the modeling effort or delegate it to others, there is no way to avoid the effects of the judgmental gap in modeling. You can ignore the problem, but that will not make the issue or its consequences disappear. Too often, organizations have used financial modeling as a surrogate for common sense in decision making. Both can be used in a synergistic way to amplify the strengths of each. More will be said on this subject in the chapter on organizational considerations.

Role of the Computer in Financial Modeling

There is considerable debate within the financial community as to the need for computer support for the modeling effort. At the present time the financial manager has a plethora of computer-usage options available. There are large mainframe computers that can support the most extensive financial modeling programs and minicomputers able to operate either in a stand-alone mode within a division or department or tied to a network of computers and their ancillary data base support. The potential of the microprocessor is enormous, because it can bring computing power to the desks of the analyst and manager. Some minicomputers are offered with program packages to perform many business and financial functions. It is not unreasonable to expect major changes in this area, and those changes will have a profound effect on the way organizations provide computer support for decision makers.

The impact of time-sharing and service bureaus is considerable, because it enables the financial manager to access large external data bases and computer programs which the firm might find too expensive to develop or maintain on its own.

Although a computer is not essential for financial modeling, it would be remiss of me not to convey the important contribution of computers to the modeling effort. They remove a great deal of the repetitive drudgery that is part of recomputing values as the model user explores different scenarios. Besides, the computer, which operates at nanosecond speed and beyond, is far better suited to calculation than human beings. Using a computer will leave far more time to the financial manager to consider alternative strategies and to close the judgmental gap discussed previously.

Is Financial Modeling an Art or a Science?

There is no question at all that modeling is both an art and a science. It is a science because successful modeling employs the scientific method throughout the process. There are techniques which are based on assumptions and have very structured procedures for their use. The individual must adhere to the requirements and assumptions of the techniques. Statistical estimation, for example, is based on a common body of knowledge which cannot be ignored.

The reader could easily be deluded into thinking that because of its highly mathematical nature, financial modeling is pure science. This is far from the truth, as some of the early failures in this area can attest.

Where exactly does the art of modeling come into play? Models are written by people and for people, and their purpose is to assist in the decision-making support function. Those factors alone should be enough to highlight why financial modeling is still an art. Knowing what the difference is between the problem and the symptom, motivating the user to provide accurate data, and fitting the model to the manager's decision-making style are all examples of the art of modeling.

To ignore either the art or the science of modeling could be fatal for an organization's modeling efforts. This book presents both elements in a balanced way. Some chapters predominantly discuss techniques with a lesser emphasis on the "art" dimension. Other chapters highlight the organizational considerations and treat the technical issues in a lesser light.

Properties of a Good Model

A fitting way to conclude this chapter is to present a set of properties by which a model could be judged. Before we do that we should address the question of why one should build a financial model.

As stated previously, people build models in order to help support the decision-making process. If the process of modeling gives the decision maker a better understanding of the risk involved in a decision and facilitates coming to a decision, then the model has value. Still, the question remains whether the cost of building, testing, and using the model is justified. In a very general sense, one can say that the modeling process was worth the effort when the value derived from the process exceeds the cost. Unfortunately, in most situations the cost side is considerably easier to measure than the value component. Let us illustrate this point with an example.

Consider a capital expenditure decision of a go/no-go variety. A model might have been developed at a cost of $75,000 to aid in the decision-making process. With or without a model, a decision will have to be made. Let us assume that the best decision was to "go." If the decision maker builds the model, incurs the cost, and makes the same decision he would have made otherwise, what is the value of the model? Zero, some people would say—a complete waste of time and money. Others would insist that the modeling effort lent objective support to their original intuitive judgment and thus gave them greater confidence in the decision. To many individuals the $75,000 cost of building the financial model was well worth it because a better understanding of the dynamics was achieved. The answer depends on the individual's attitude toward risk and perceived benefit received.

The key point is that the expenditure on modeling should always be viewed in the light of alternative uses for the funds. Is this the most effective. way to allocate my resources? Some managers believe financial modeling is cost-effective while others do not. Hopefully, this book will increase the awareness levels of both types so that financial modeling efforts are deployed to reap the greatest benefits possible.

But let's return to the properties of a good model, whether purchased or developed especially by the user's organization. Here they are:

○ *Simplicity*—a model should refrain from unnecessary complexity.

- ○ *Conversationality*—the financial manager should be able to interact with the model in as English-like a manner as possible.
- ○ *Flexibility*—the values of the model (estimates and assumptions) should be easily modified to reflect changes in the environment.
- ○ *Completeness*—the model should capture the essence of reality.
- ○ *Expansion/Contraction*—the manager should be able to expand or contract the scope of the model depending on circumstances. If an in-depth analysis is needed for a decision, a model is refined to include greater coverage. However, if a review of the situation dictates a reduction in model size, this should not result in major problems.

Although there are many more properties that a financial model could possess, these are certainly sufficient to serve as a starting point in assessing the quality of a model. The reader should recall that most decision situations are characterized by time pressure and limited resources, including information. Attempting to develop too elaborate a model might indeed result in a sophisticated model—too late to be of use. On the other hand, a simplistic, piecemeal model might be ready on time but misleading. A balance must be struck among the properties discussed previously. That is part of the art of modeling.

2

Some Insights into Financial Forecasting Models

WE begin our presentation of modeling with a discussion of forecasting models because good financial decision making is so dependent on the development of a good forecast. Regardless of the level of sophistication of our model, a forecast of key variables is always one of the first problems that will have to be faced.

The purpose of this chapter is to present to the financial manager a methodology for dealing with the difficult task of developing a forecast to drive the other components of the financial model. The next chapter will present some specific forecasting techniques which the reader may find useful in developing a forecast. The reader who is not interested in specific forecasting techniques can skip the next chapter and still not experience a loss in the continuity of the book.

Must We Forecast?

Every time we develop a plan or engage in the budgeting process we must forecast. Often, initial values are used to represent starting points so that we may continue with the rest of the process. The fact of the matter is that we forecast all the time. Sometimes we do it explicitly in a more formal manner; other times we do it implicitly, using values derived without a great deal of thought. Either way we forecast.

In Chapter 1 we defined a financial model as a symbolic representation of a financial situation. In particular, a model is based on variables interrelated by mathematical relationships. Estimates of the values of the variables were required. How we derive these estimates and use them to deal with future situations is the central issue in forecasting. What makes this so challenging is that we forecast future events, for which there are no data. What we usually have, or can obtain with some effort, are data on the past. Which items are relevant to aid us in forecasting a future event is also a key question that must be addressed in forecasting.

Approaches to Forecasting

Managers use many different approaches to cope with the challenge of forecasting. We can group these approaches into two broad categories: qualitative procedures and quantitative procedures. Very little can be said about pure qualitative forecasting except that the larger an organization becomes, the less likely it is to use this type of approach. The nature of corporate decision making is characterized by analysis and review, and a completely qualitative approach to forecasting will be difficult to justify by superiors. Just imagine for a moment a president of a utility company appearing before a regulating hearing saying that the pending request for a rate increase was based on a "feeling" that the estimates presented were to occur. I am not saying that there is no place for subjectivity in forecasting, but there must be some balance between more analytical procedures and common sense.

Quantitative procedures are based on an empirical analysis of data. The nature of the data selected determines the type of quantitative approach that will be followed. The forecasting procedure perhaps used most frequently by financial managers is some type of extrapolation of historical data. These data can be drawn from a company's data base and might be available for several past periods. Data that are sequenced by time are referred to as a *time series*. An example of a time series for sales is:

Year	Sales (000)
1980	$725
1979	715
1978	701
1977	684
1976	652

One of the problems with using a time series is obtaining a sufficient number of past data points. Many of the techniques require considerable amounts of such historical data. Another problem is the "staleness" of historical data. Just how relevant are data about the past to a company engaged in a highly evolving industry? Building a financial forecasting model using historical data is as much an art as it is a science. In the following chapter we will outline several methods for conducting an analysis of time series data.

Many companies recognize that they are not considering all the available information when they use simple extrapolation methods to forecast future values for the key variables in their models. Quite often a financial manager has an idea that certain variables have some influence on the behavior of the key variable for which a forecast is to be developed. Without realizing it, the manager is developing a working hypothesis, which is subject to empirical verification through readily available statistical procedures. The next step for our manager would be to establish the direction of influence—in other words, determine exactly which variables influence our target variable, and in what way. Before we get too involved in the mechanics, suffice it to say that this type of forecasting procedure is known as the development of *causal models*. Some of the more sophisticated financial modeling packages on the market have the capability for dealing with the type of relationships derived from causal models. Many, however, do not.

Let us return to the financial manager who has identified several key variables as possible explanatory factors for the target variable. It is entirely possible that some of the data are not available within the firm's internal time-series data base. An example might be the disposable personal income per capita for the last ten years. In most cases, such information can be found in some table in a book in a library somewhere. The point I am trying to make is that a financial forecasting model of any degree of sophistication typically makes use of some data readily available within the firm's data base and some data that must be obtained from external sources.

Selecting appropriate external variables to be tested in a company's financial forecasting model could easily involve a time-consuming and error-prone search procedure. Most companies engaged in financial model building have found it beneficial to subscribe to external economic data bases, which are available from many time-sharing companies. A casual review of the data bases available leads one to the immediate conclusion that it would be wasteful to subscribe to all of them. Many of these data bases are specifically related to an industry, such as oil or publishing, while others contain general economic data as provided, for example, by Citibank or Data Resources, Inc.

The reader should be cautioned that not all data bases are available from all vendors, so some type of needs analysis should be performed. A financial manager could find himself using a data base from one vendor and a financial modeling package from a different vendor. Some provision would be necessary to integrate the two applications. It is not uncommon for a single company to be associated with several vendors in order to meet all the requirements of the financial modeling effort.

One should keep in mind that every time data are accessed and/or stored in their files, a charge is incurred for time-sharing usage. This can become quite expensive in the early exploratory stages of the development of a financial forecasting model when a great deal of time is spent testing several plausible hypotheses. This testing process is facilitated by the presence of a battery of statistical techniques and hardware support. Since most time-sharing vendors and other sources provide the programs to do the analysis of the data, the casual reader might assume that the task of forecasting should be easy. Far from the truth! Every statistical technique is based on a given set of assumptions which, if violated, can undermine the success of the forecasting effort. The problem lies with the user who has this vast array of computational power at his disposal and is freed from doing the onerous calculations. All that is needed, it seems, is a data base, packaged software, and a communications capability. With the effort of typing a line, a forecast can be generated. Whether or not proper statistical procedures were followed, an impressive-looking computer printout is generated. The fact that it can be based on incorrect assumptions and procedures is what makes it imperative to have competent people conducting your modeling activity.

Most financial model builders simply do not have the statistical knowledge to cope with the myriad problems that could surface in employing many of the statistical techniques, particulary some of the more exotic ones being marketed today.

Here is where proper documentation and technical support become so important to the model builder. If a question arises about the proper use of a technique and the documentation is not completely clear, then your last resource is the technical support specialist. Most of these support people know how to help you put data into the proper form so that it can be accepted by the computer program. Unfortunately, what many of them do not know is how to use the specific technique in a methodologically correct way. The real victim is the financial model builder who assumes that everything is being done correctly. The obvious result could be an incorrect forecast that might be an important component of the whole modeling effort.

Interactive Financial Forecasting

Most organizations using financial modeling have found that interactive methods can be extremely productive. In this mode, the analyst communicates with the computer programs in a conversational manner using either a hard-copy printer terminal or a visual display device. This is a vast improvement over methods that rely on a batch mode of processing, in which delays of a day or more between processing forecast models are not uncommon. Unfortunately, there are some operational limitations of interactive forecasting procedures.

Earlier in this chapter we discussed the enormous power available to the forecaster as a result of the numerous pro-grammed techniques and data bases that are available. The presence of high-powered software and hardware allows a model builder to generate a forecast on the basis of what I will call robot data-screening procedures. In this type of situation the financial analyst requests that the computer routines scan the data base and, on the basis of statistical association, extract what appears to be patterns within the data. Once the patterns are identified, a hypothesis is sought which purports to explain the behavior of the data. It should be obvious to the reader, in the light of the discussion of the previous section, how this kind of procedure can be abused by a poorly qualified model builder. I have personally witnessed, on numerous occasions, individuals trying to use these procedures in their forecasting programs and committing major errors in the interpretation of the results. When an analyst is working in this area, he is truly engaged in the art, rather than the science, of modeling.

Another very serious error made by many people engaged in building financial forecasting models is the improper use of default options that are contained in many of the statistical programs. A default option occurs when the model builder fails to enter a value for a parameter that is requested by a computer program. In such a situation the computer defaults to a predetermined value that is usually stated somewhere in the program's documentation manual. In many situations the inexperienced user elects the default value when it is entirely inappropriate in the given application. Once again, results are generated that look O.K. but are incorrect.

As a general rule, I have found, the more complicated the statistical procedure is, the more likely it is that the vendor has programmed numerous default options. Why is this the case? So that it is "easier" to use. Whether or not it is used properly is left to the good judgment of the individual model builder, as it should be. Any vendor that tried to build in controls on the use of the particular package would be at a severe disadvantage in the marketplace. The only resolution to this dilemma is to proceed with extreme caution in using quantitative forecasting procedures, recognize your limitations (we all have some), and call for special assistance when it is appropriate. Some of the larger organizations that have been modeling for some time have recognized this problem and have established a technical support staff to handle just such contingencies. Smaller organizations and firms just getting started in financial modeling must seek the advice of their technical support representatives or call for the services of an outside consultant.

What Is a Good Forecast?

We stated earlier in this chapter that regardless of the degree of sophistication of the financial model, we all must forecast financial variables. The key question that must be answered is how much better is my forecast going to be if I use a more sophisticated process to determine it? Once again, the guide line should be whether or not the value derived by the better forecast exceeds the cost incurred.

It is a generally accepted principle that, all things being equal, short-term forecasting tends to be more accurate than long-term forecasting. The farther out into the future we try to forecast, the less accurate we can expect our forecast to be. In short-term economic forecasts we generally assume that the conditions which existed in the past will be continued in the future, whereas with long-term forecasts we challenge the stability of the support structure of the environment that is being forecasted.

The general procedure for measuring the accuracy of a forecast is to compute the deviation of the forecasted value from the actual value. The objective is to keep the aggregate measure of the deviations as small as resources will permit. Statisticians have developed rather precise measures to compare the accuracy of one method's forecast with that of another.

There are two very important points that should be kept in mind when evaluating a financial forecasting procedure. The first is that a forecast will rarely hit the target exactly. A model builder can concentrate his efforts either on the forecast itself or on the tracking mechanism so that, as new information comes into the firm, an adjusted forecast based on the new information can be computed. I like to use the analogy of the play of a centerfielder in baseball. One person might try to play every batter in a different position and spend a great deal of time analyzing all the variables, such as pitcher, wind conditions, and so forth, and position himself (forecast) in just the right spot. Another player might play every batter in exactly the same spot and rely on his legs (corrective action) to get to where the ball was hit (actual value). The proper approach is to have an effective forecasting system and the ability to gather and analyze new data to correct for any previous errors in judgment.

The second important point to remember in generating a financial forecast is to generate not one but two numbers. These numbers should represent a target value and a deviation, which could be either plus or minus some percentage. This recognizes the fact that perfect accuracy is rarely achieved. You convey more information to the manager if you present your financial forecast as a range. This point will be developed further in the chapter on sensitivity analysis. Suffice it to say that when it comes time to enter the forecast into the financial model, it is possible to test the effects of different points of the range on the indicated measures of effectiveness.

Recent years have proven that many patterns that existed in the past and which provided aid to the forecaster simply do not appear to exist anymore. This phenomenon places added pressure on the financial model builder to look for new relationships which might exist and to monitor their behavior continuously so that the mistakes of the past are not repeated again in the future.

Summary

In this chapter we have presented some of the key points in developing forecasts for financial models. We described the two types of forecasting approaches—qualitative and quantitative. The differences between extrapolation methods and causal methods were presented. The significance of external data bases was discussed along with important user caveats. The role of assumptions underlying the various statistical techniques was pointed out, with special consideration given to the dangers inherent in using the computer improperly. We concluded the chapter with a discussion on what is a good forecast.

In the next chapter we present a brief description of some of the more widely used techniques for forecasting key variables in financial modeling.

3

Overview of Forecasting Methods

THE purpose of this chapter is to describe in a nontechnical manner the essential characteristics of some readily available forecasting techniques. The reader who is not interested in this exposition can skip this chapter without experiencing a loss in continuity.

The first step that should be taken after identifying what you believe are the key variables in your forecast is to collect the data for those variables and have them readily available on a computer file. Figure 1 illustrates a time series for a plausible variable of interest to a modeler for a publishing firm. Additional data on other relevant variables could be obtained in a similar manner. Before proceeding to establish the existence of any statistical relationship, the forecaster must take special care to ensure the correctness and completeness of the data. Errors arising from data entry should be corrected and the data reentered, and proper procedures for coping with missing data elements should be followed.

Most computer packages have the capability to plot the data. Many forecasters request a plot of each of the data series before selecting a given forecasting technique. The plot of the data series gives the analyst a visual method for detecting the presence of underlying patterns within the data. A trained analyst can use the information gained from the plot to select an appropriate forecasting strategy.

Figure I. Time series for book sales.

Month	*Sales (000)*	*Month*	*Sales (000)*
Jan. 1974	$121	Nov. 1974	$326
Feb. 1974	154	Dec. 1974	291
Mar. 1974	234	Jan. 1975	317
Apr. 1974	289	Feb. 1975	274
May 1974	262	Mar. 1975	279
Jun. 1974	308	Apr. 1975	210
Jul. 1974	193	May 1975	224
Aug. 1974	324	Jun. 1975	218
Sep. 1974	335	Jul. 1975	129
Oct. 1974	341	Aug. 1975	157

Figure 2 contains a typical plot of monthly sales data which was generated by a standard hard-copy computer terminal. Figure 3 shows the same type of data, but this time a standard flatbed plotter device was used. In many instances the graph generated in Figure 2 is more than adequate for the initial data screening application. However, if presentations are to be made to financial management, then a graph as depicted in Figure 3 is more appropriate.

It is relatively easy to extract data from files and report them in the form of tables or attractive computer-generated graphs. At this point the forecaster must decide on the type of

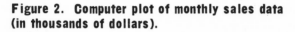

Figure 2. Computer plot of monthly sales data (in thousands of dollars).

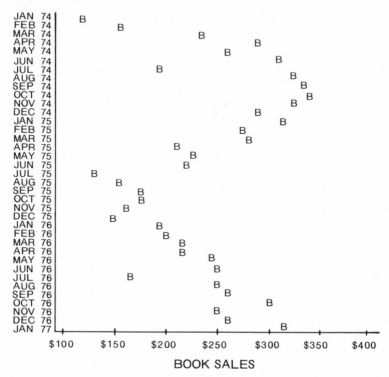

forecasting procedure that is most appropriate to the forecast objective and the task at hand. This is a good time to review the caveats expressed in the previous chapter.

Simple or Naive Forecasting Models

The first type of forecasting model that will be discussed is the one based on a time series. Recall that a time series for one or more variables is an ordered sequence of values that have

Figure 3. Improved computer plot of sales data (in thousands of dollars)

meaning only when in their proper order. Examples of time series are sales by month for several years and quarterly values for the GNP for the past ten years. The former is an example of a business series, whereas the latter represents a time series of external general economic data. Both types of data series are invaluable to the financial forecaster.

Quite often the model builder relies on naive (overly simple) forecasting approaches to provide data for input to financial models. For one reason or another, the financial analyst might be content to rely on a method which takes past values and adjusts them by a percentage increase or decrease based on intuitive judgment. Very little quantitative analysis is involved, and there is no attempt to analytically seek out structural components of data. The percentage increase or decrease might have growth or contraction rates explicitly incorporated into the estimates.

Most financial modeling systems on the market permit the model builder to override formal statistical forecasting procedures and to enter a manual forecast or to substitute one of the more simple approaches. The degree to which this is facilitated is what was meant in the first chapter when we discussed properties of a good financial model. Many model builders look condescendingly on naive forecasting procedures, but many financial managers are less comfortable with the use of anything more mathematical or sophisticated. It is the responsibility of the analyst to demonstrate to the financial manager that a given technique is a more effective forecasting device than the one that is currently being used. If this cannot be done, why should the financial manager be expected to change his or her adopted method of forecasting? People resist doing things that to them are unnatural and not demonstrated to be of value. Here is where a combination of technical knowledge and communications skill pays off for the model builder.

Decomposition Methods

The premise behind the decomposition methods of forecasting is that any time series is composed of four components: seasonal factors, cyclical factors, trend factors, and a random or irregular term. These elements differ in their duration and consistency within a given series. The purpose of decomposition procedures is to identify and extract the individual and combined effects of these components and to use that information in generating forecasts for the future behavior of the variable under consideration.

Several decomposition methods exist, and each one provides one or more additional features that might prove to be of value to the financial forecaster. In each case extreme care is needed in interpreting the output generated by the computer programs. At the very least, some degree of statistical training is a necessity in order to use decomposition methods effectively.

It should be noted that decomposition methods differ from the approaches mentioned in the previous section in that they assume that a series of underlying patterns is present in the past data and will continue in the future. Capitalizing on the knowledge of these patterns to generate better forecasts is the whole basis for the analysis. This notion of stability in the behavior of the variable over time is perhaps the most important ingredient in all time-series approaches to forecasting. If the model builder has reason to believe that some forces, both internal or external to the organization, are at work changing the underlying patterns, then serious consideration should be given to other approaches that are not based on such constraining conditions. Nevertheless, decomposition methods are used quite often in analyzing time-series data to generate input values as forecasts for financial models.

Averages and Smoothing Techniques

Most financial managers realize that many forces interact to influence the level of a key variable that they are attempting to forecast and use as input to a financial model. Many internal and/or external events can cause any one specific data element to be unduly influenced. This can occur if our data point represents a day, week, month, quarter, or even a year. The coping mechanism which is frequently used is to take an average of past values. This action, it is believed, will counteract the highs and lows and eventually even them out.

Perhaps the greatest defense of the use of the simple average is that it is easily understood, but blind use of this or any statistical procedure is one of the surest ways to fail in forecasting.

There are three major types of averages used in forecasting: simple, weighted, and moving averages. The simple average does not have the ability to "move through time," and this severely limits its use. In order to compensate for this shortcoming, the moving-average procedure was developed. This technique utilizes a number of past values of a variable and then computes the average to serve as a forecast for the next period. The procedure is updated for the next period by excluding the oldest data point and adding the immediately preceding actual value. This rolling forecast enables new information to be added while older and presumably less valuable data are deleted.

Aside from data storage considerations, the central operating question for the successful use of the moving-average technique is how long the period of the cycle should be. A six-month moving average carries six months of data, whereas a three-month moving average carries only three. The selection of a period dramatically influences the ability of the forecast to cope with the effects of seasons, cycles, and trend components. It also determines the responsiveness of the forecast to irregular or shock effects such as sudden increase or decrease in demand for a product due to weather conditions or a strike.

A key assumption of the moving average is that every past data value is to be given equal weight in determining the forecast for the coming period. For example, a four-month moving average implies that an equal weight of 0.25 is given to each past month. A ten-month moving average implies an equal weight of 0.10, and so on. The fact that older data might have become a bit stale is ignored by the methodology of the moving average.

A great deal of theoretical work has been done to examine the behavior of the moving-average model under different conditions of perturbation. Suffice it to say that unless adjustments are made to the average, the approach will yield a forecast that tends to lag behind any underlying changes that have occurred in the operating environment. The severity of the lag can be directly traced to the period chosen for the moving-average model by the forecaster.

In order to compensate for the problems created by the equal weighting inherent in the moving-average model, forecasters have elected to use a weighted moving-average model. In this approach, the forecaster determines the length of period in the same manner as in the moving-average approach. However, instead of being restricted to equal weights for the past data values, the model builder is permitted to establish a weighting scheme according to his subjective assessment of the rate of deterioration of past data. In this way newer data can be weighted to reflect a greater impact on the forecast for the next period. There still remains the need to select a forecasting period and determine the weights. After a period of experimentation the financial model builder will settle on a set of weights with which he can be comfortable. Subjective weighting is one of the principal considerations which makes the weighted moving average appealing. As a general rule the simpler the approach the more appealing it will be to the financial manager. Recall our discussion in Chapter 1 regarding properties of a good model.

Exponential Smoothing

Another example of a univariate (one-variable) forecasting technique which has attracted widespread interest and use in time-series forecasting is exponential smoothing. The basic premise of this technique is that newer or more recent data values are assigned a greater weight. The difference between this and the weighted moving-average method is the manner in which the weights are assigned. The weights are assigned to yield the equations that best fit the past data. The forecaster may guess at an initial value or may use a computer program that estimates the weights directly.

In exponential smoothing, each new forecast is derived

from the previous forecast by adjusting for a factor reflecting the error from the previous forecast. The financial forecaster has three types of exponential smoothing models from which to choose: single, double, and triple. The choice of the model depends on an analysis of the nature of the data and whether or not a trend or growth component is present. Single exponential smoothing is most effective when the time series is stationary. Double exponential smoothing is appropriate when the data contain a linear trend. Triple exponential smoothing models are used to forecast nonlinear trends in the time series. The procedures of decomposition can be used to incorporate seasonal factors in the forecast.

The analyst must select or estimate one or more smoothing constants, which serve as the set of weights to be used in the forecasting model. The use of this smoothing constant serves as an example of the use of the default option in a computer program. The forecaster can insert what he believes to be an appropriate smoothing constant, or he can let the exponential smoothing program estimate the parameters which best fit the past data in the sense that a specified deviation is minimal. As in all time-series procedures, the implicit assumption is that the patterns of the past as reflected in the data series will continue into the future.

The most troublesome issue confronting the user of an exponential forecasting model is the selection of the smoothing constant. Once again, the best approach is a combination of the artistic and the scientific sides of model building.

Adaptive Forecasting Techniques

As stated previously, an effective tracking mechanism is a most important component in any forecasting system. A forecasting model which uses current information to adapt to the changing environment—that is, which incorporates a tracking mechanism—is said to be built on *adaptive forecasting techniques.* This class of time-series forecasting techniques is somewhat more complex than the methods previously discussed in this chapter. They can be used for many of the forecasting approaches which we discussed earlier. Although there are organizations actively involved in using some of these techniques and they are heavily marketed by some time-sharing firms, the majority of financial applications does not employ them. Part of the reason is that they are not widely understood even by the vendors' technical support staffs. Another major drawback to the use of these techniques is that a large number of data points are required for them to generate accurate forecasts. All too often in a business application in the financial area it is not possible to obtain the necessary data to mount a serious attempt at using one of the more sophisticated forecasting techniques. In most situations involving time-series forecasting, a simpler model is often more than adequate for the purposes at hand, and therefore the extra cost and effort involved in building a sophisticated model are not justifiable.

Apart from these problems, there is the added difficulty of having to communicate to financial managers how the forecast was derived. As you get involved in the more esoteric forecasting techniques, greater effort in documentation and communication places an additional burden on the all-around skills of the financial modeling team. For these reasons, adaptive forecasting, at least for some time to come, will remain a matter for the specialist. The typical financial model builder, even with computer support, is cautioned to go slowly in trying to use these techniques.

Causal Models

The other major approach to develop a financial forecasting model is through causal models. With these models the forecaster seeks out to forecast target or criterion variables on the basis of one or more explanatory variables. The major examples of this type of forecasting technique are single-equation regression models and econometric models. The former category is typically represented by either bivariate linear regression or multivariate linear regression model formulations.

Perhaps the term causal models needs additional explanation. As discussed in Chapter 2, a causal model involves identifying the major variables that affect a target variable to be forecasted. A working hypothesis guides the model builder in the choice of one model form or another. The hypothesized relationship is challenged empirically by means of the data during the parameter estimation phase of the project. On the basis of the results of the initial forecasts, the forecaster refines his model until he has sufficient confidence in its ability to be used in the financial model. Underlying the model development is the belief that the explanatory variables influence or cause certain outcome values of the criterion or target variable. This notion of causality is, or should be, restricted to a statistical sense. All we can expect from a statistical procedure is to support or challenge our underlying hypothesis of the way reality works. One should not expect a procedure to *prove* causality. All too often a novice statistician is heard stating that he has proved that a certain relationship exists. Competent statisticians, particularly in their capacity as consultants to the financial model builder, are always guarded in the comments they will offer regarding the results from a statistical analysis.

Causal models have been abused by financial model builders who have ignored proper operating procedures in the use of these techniques. Most available statistical packages neglect to inform the user of the importance of adhering to the assumptions of the techniques. All too often variables are dropped from further analysis because the model builder concluded that "no relationship exists between the variables under

Figure 4. Examples of nonlinear relationships.

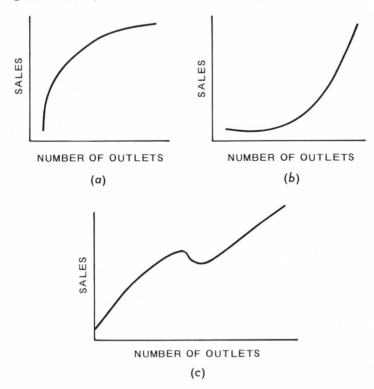

review." What should have been stated was that "no *linear* relationship exists between the two variables." Figure 4 depicts some classic examples of nonlinear relationships. Frame *(a)* represents a function which is increasing at a decreasing rate, frame *(b)* represents a function which is increasing at an increasing rate, and frame *(c)* depicts a more complex nonlinear relationship. Had the model builder been aware that the model was based on a linear relationship, he might never have come to the conclusion that was arrived at.

This is but one example from many that could be selected

to demonstrate the importance of knowing the assumptions behind a procedure. As stated earlier in this book, the availability of on-line computer programs for statistical techniques places an even greater responsibility on the financial manager to ensure that the modeling team possesses an adequate degree of competence in the techniques being used. Since most financial managers do not possess this competence themselves, trust between the model builder and the financial manager becomes all the more important.

No discussion of this subject will be complete without relating causal models to the state of the art in financial modeling. Virtually all time-sharing vendors supply statistical packages that handle the techniques we have presented. The same thing can be said for mainframe manufacturers. Therefore, the software to perform the analysis is readily available. The key issue is not availability per se but what the user must be expected to do to use these procedures effectively.

A vast majority of the financial modeling software, as the industry perceives it, is not capable of adequately interfacing with the models discussed in this section. Only the more powerful financial modeling systems give the financial manager the capability of using econometric modeling techniques. Some of those systems still expect a great deal of sophistication on the part of the user. The degree of "conversationality" of some of these systems leaves a great deal to be desired. What then can the model builder expect as he tries to evaluate different modeling systems with regard to their capability to support a serious financial forecasting program? Variety! Many systems make no explicit provision for anything but the entry of a single number entered manually, whereas other systems provide an elaborate mechanism to interface a wide variety of forecasting techniques with the actual financial model logic. This interface can and should be expected to be written in as conversational a style as possible. If the average financial organization is to make effective use of financial forecasting systems, then the burden must be placed on the vendors to provide software that is user-oriented and not technician-oriented. At the present time, few systems can really be said to approach this level.

Summary

In this chapter we have examined the major types of financial forecasting techniques used in organizations. The more elementary forecasting techniques included extrapolation, decomposition methods, moving averages, and exponential smoothing. We also considered more sophisticated methods known as adaptive forecasting techniques. The remainder of the chapter was devoted to issues in using causal models in forecasting.

Throughout this presentation we have avoided the technical details upon which the various approaches to forecasting are based. Instead our emphasis was on the major considerations of interest to the financial model builder who has a limited technical background. The interested reader can pursue the technical points at leisure. For the individual who is getting started in financial modeling it is imperative to be aware of the various types of forecasting techniques that are available and the major pitfalls that await careless users. I hope that after reading this chapter the reader will approach the task of forecasting with a new awareness of the opportunities successful modeling can provide.

4

Optimization Procedures in Financial Modeling

IN deciding on the topics to be covered in a book on getting started in financial modeling, the one that I had the most difficulty with was this chapter on optimization procedures. The basic dilemma arises from the fact that some financial model builders themselves do not feel that optimization has any place at all in the discussion. They argue that no one they know of is using optimization and that most packages have absolutely no optimization capabilities. These statements are correct as far as they go, but they do not tell the complete story. Let us review what is meant by an optimization model.

Some Basic Facts about Optimization Procedures

A financial manager is interested in developing a model to assist in the decision-making process. Following the procedure outlined in an earlier chapter, the analyst identifies the key variables that are believed to influence the decision situation. One or more outcome measures are determined to be appropriate for judging the efficacy of the choice situation surrounding a particular decision. The traditional term for these measures is objective functions. The attainment of a desirable level of performance of an objective function is usually limited by a series of constraints on various variables that may or may not be under the control of the decision maker. Exactly how many of these restraints are incorporated into the model depends completely on the ability of the financial analyst to recognize their existence and then to formulate a mathematical statement of the relationships. It is quite obvious that a model builder who lacks the understanding of the environment under review is at a severe disadvantage when it comes to formulating the essential constraint equations. The reader should appreciate the key trade-off considerations of having technically trained specialists versus financially knowledgeable people serving on the modeling team.

Once we have identified the key variables and hypothesized plausible relationships among them, we can construct a verbal model of our view of the situation. The exact functional form of our objective function and the constraining relations have not been determined as yet. What usually happens at this stage when our verbal model is reviewed is that we realize that some important variables or relationships have been omitted and others are redundant. This leads to a refinement of the verbal model, a process which allows the participants in the modeling project to explore the boundaries of the decision support system that is being proposed. The modeling team might expand the model to include areas previously declared not relevant to the project. Likewise, entire portions of the model could be eliminated from further refinement because of the realization that the effort would not be relevant or cost-effective. It is usually beneficial to have all key personnel provide their input at this time, because the more perspectives are considered, the more insights will be offered. In addition, it is less likely that important components of the model will be overlooked.

Armed with a verbal model of a financial decision situation, the model builder must convert the words to mathematical relationships. Two basic types of relationships are employed at this time: definitional equations and behavioral functions. Examples of definitional equations are "assets equal liabilities plus net worth" and "beginning inventory equals ending inventory plus receipts minus withdrawals." This type of relationship is important throughout the financial area. Major examples that come to mind are budgets, balance sheets, and profit-and-loss statements. An example of a behavioral function is the functional relationship between sales of automobiles and the state of the economy. In this case we attempt to formulate a functional relationship and estimate the parameters. In effect, the proposed relationship is tested empirically in much the same way as are forecasting models (see Chapter 3).

At this point in the model-building process we must anticipate a certain amount of difficulty. Data collection is needed to develop an adequate data base on certain variables so that we can provide reasonably accurate estimates of their true values. We must rely on statistical estimation procedures where appropriate and, at times, use our best judgment when insufficient data are available.

Slowly, ever so slowly, our model begins to take shape. Each equation is formulated, tested, and evaluated in light of the availability of our existing resources. At some point, the verbal model has been transformed into a mathematical statement of the financial decision under review.

The modeling team studies the resulting set of relationships and tries to detect the presence of patterns. What is the nature of the mathematical relationships? Are they linear? Do we have several objective functions or only one? Can the variables take on any values, or must they be restricted to integer values? (For example, a firm can have five or six warehouses but not five and one-half.) The answers to these and other similar questions have a tremendous impact on the next step in the model-building process.

There are prepackaged solution procedures, called algorithms, which are readily available to form the basis for solutions to well-known model formulations. If the modeling team recognizes that the situation being modeled has certain characteristics of prototype model formulations, then an attempt can be made to use the appropriate solution methodologies. Typically, some compromise must be made between the realism of the model and the computational requirements of certain model formulations. In other words, the modeling team might decide that even though the functional relationships being investigated are not exactly of the form required by a solution procedure, they should be modified, or "idealized," so that they possess the appropriate characteristics.

Here is where the judgmental gap becomes so important. Whenever compromises of this type must be made, the decision maker must be made aware of the effect that force fitting has on the final solution produced by the model. In many situations the problem is not so severe as it appears, because sensitivity analysis can be used to make up for the distortion. This topic will be discussed in a later chapter.

The reader might legitimately ask why a modeling team would even consider making these compromises. The answer lies in the fact that optimization model formulations often generate optimal solutions to a given situation. An optimal solution is defined as the best possible mix of values for the decision variables, given the nature of the constraining relations of the model. Note, though, that what is generated is the optimal solution to the formulated model and not necessarily the optimal solution to the real-world financial decision.

Not every modeling team proceeds in the fashion outlined in this chapter. Quite often it has a preconceived idea as to the type of model it is going to develop. Rather than spend time on considering the pros and cons of an optimization formulation, some teams ignore this type of solution procedure completely. Why is this so? The major reason is that developing optimization models requires a substantially greater technical knowledge than developing either report generators or simulations. Another reason is that the early developers of financial models using optimization methods had some rather highly visible failures. These failures resulted not so much from the methodology as from organizational difficulties, which are discussed elsewhere in this book. Lofty promises were made that could not be met. It is interesting to note that while optimization procedures have achieved minimal successes in financial decision situations, they have been widely adopted in other application areas in business.

It is my opinion that for properly trained model builders, optimization models can be a welcome addition to the modeling arsenal. The key point is to assess the appropriateness of the application and ensure that a useful model is developed in a cost-effective manner.

When one considers building a financial model based on the optimization approach, it is important to realize that there is no "package." The modeling team formulates a model as described in the preceding section and then determines whether or not it can be accommodated by one of the standard solution procedures. Most of the computer programs written for this area revolve around the use of algorithms. These algorithms accept data and set about to solve the formulated model for the optimal value of the objective function. The software that is required to support optimization models is very sophisticated. The companies which provide this software also provide extensive, highly technical consulting services. I would like to warn against some vendors who claim that their companies provide optimization software. What they actually have are pedagogical or "toy" versions, which are used primarily by colleges and universities as teaching devices. The real production algorithms make much more efficient use of computer resources and can solve extremely large realistic models.

One of the major problems encountered in the successful use of optimization models is data input and solution output. The vast volume of data involved has necessitated the incorporation of efficient provisions for matrix and report generation. In fact, any evaluation of optimization software should pay as much attention to input/output considerations as to the actual solution procedure itself. Vendors of these systems provide extensive training on the efficient use of their systems. Suffice it to say that any model-building group considering the use of optimization modeling should be careful to weigh the cost of establishing the required internal expertise against the use of less complex approaches.

The next section of this chapter will discuss some of the more readily available types of optimization models.

Optimization Models and Mathematical Programming

Whenever one speaks of optimization methods in model building, the class of algorithms known as mathematical programming models comes directly to the forefront. Each model type has an objective function and constraining relationships similar to those described earlier in this chapter. The functional form of the mathematical relationship is what differentiates one mathematical programming model from another type. We will present and discuss some of the more useful forms of this class of model so that the financial analyst can become familiar with them and can better evaluate their potential for future use in his own organization.

Linear Programming Models

The most widely used mathematical programming models are of the linear programming variety. Early optimization models using linear programming were supposed to assist in decisions supporting the corporate effort. Linear programming models can be independent or they can be embedded in a larger modeling effort, where they serve as a module for a much larger system.

The name linear programming comes from the fact that all functional relationships (that is, the objective function and all constraints) are of the linear type. An example of a linear equation is

$$z = 27 + 52x + 19y$$

The key concept that must be appreciated is that in linear programming, variables cannot be related in other than a linear fashion. Therefore, as the financial modeling team moves from verbal model to a mathematical statement of the problem, care must be taken to determine whether or not the functional relationships are indeed linear. During parameter estimation the model builder is able to assess whether or not a linear programming formulation is a plausible approach.

In order to give the reader a feel for the implications of linear models, we will discuss the assumptions behind all linear programming models.

First, the solution values for decision variables are permitted to take on fractional values. Another key assumption of linear programming models is based on the concept of constant returns to scale. The linear model implies that a doubling of the input factor will have a proportionate impact on the output factor. Obviously, there are many real-world situations where this is not the case. However, within acceptable ranges the assumption could be valid for some variables.

The linear programming model assumes *additivity* of the modeled processes—that is, that output from one process can be combined with output from another process as long as the items are of the same type.

From our brief discussion of these assumptions it should be clear to the reader that there are many situations where a linear programming formulation for a financial model is inappropriate. A skilled model builder can sometimes "trick" the solution algorithm by formulating relationships that are linear but are actually transformations of what are basically nonlinear phenomena. However, this is beyond what can be expected of the average individual engaged in financial modeling.

What makes linear optimization models so appealing to model builders is the existence of a very efficient solution algorithm, known as the simplex method. It is not our purpose in this section to discuss the solution procedure employed in the simplex algorithm but simply to inform the reader that it is available and forms the basis of all commercially available mathematical programming systems. If a solution to a linear programming model exists, then the simplex procedure guarantees that an optimal solution will be found. That is the *raison d'être* of an optimization algorithm. We will see later in this chapter that there are other forms of mathematical programming model types which do not have such an algorithm.

Integer Programming Models

The financial modeling team will often encounter situations for which the assumptions of linear programming models are not appropriate. Notably, this occurs when there is an additional requirement that one or more of the decision variables must be restricted to integer values. The financial analyst can easily think of several situations where this would be the case.

There are at least two ways of proceeding in this type of situation. The financial model builder could develop a linear programming model and attempt to solve the model without explicitly considering any of the integer restrictions that are deemed pertinent. In that case, the model results are reviewed and rounded up to yield the integer values of the decision variables. In certain types of situations this may pose no problem as long as the model builder is assured that a valid solution results, in particular, that the informal adjustment of some values does not violate some of the constraining relations. Unless special care is taken, checking the implications of the changes on a large-scale model could be impossible. Remember our earlier discussion of the judgmental gap. This is a perfect example of the need to subjectively filter the model results before they are used for decision making.

The second approach open to the model builder is to use an integer programming model formulation directly. Before attempting to solve the model, it is essential to determine precisely which variables will be required to take integer values. If all the variables are made integer, then we have what is called a pure integer programming model. If some of the decision variables are restricted to be integer and others are not, we have what is referred to as a mixed integer linear programming problem. A useful rule of thumb to follow is that the number of variables with an integer restriction should be kept as small as possible. Adding integer-restricted variables to a model that are not really necessary simply adds to the overhead costs without providing truly useful information to the decision maker.

The reader may be interested to know that the integer programming solution procedures are intrinsically tied to the linear programming procedure described in the previous section. There are many interesting types of problems that could be solved using integer linear programming procedures. The interested reader is directed to one of the many textbooks which have been written on the subject. Some warning is in order because the mathematical level of most of the expositions on integer programming models is enough to challenge even the dedicated reader.

Nonlinear Programming Models

As the name implies, this class of mathematical programming models involves nonlinear functional relationships. These nonlinear relationships can appear in the objective function or in the constraining relations, or in both.

In the case of linear programming models there is a general-purpose optimization algorithm. This is not the case with nonlinear programming models. Specific solution algorithms have been developed for a limited number of types of nonlinear models. The model builder who formulates a nonlinear model must investigate whether or not there exists a usable solution algorithm. Even if an algorithm is available, there often is no guarantee that a true optimal solution will be generated. What sometimes happens is that the computer software "believes" that it has found an optimal solution. It is with modeling of this kind that one truly experiences the art of modeling. Ingenuity is required not only to formulate an accurate model but also to ensure that the solution obtained is appropriate.

The reader might wonder at this point why anyone would even care to use nonlinear models in his work. The answer lies in the fact that many real-world phenomena can only be modeled using nonlinear relationships. The richness of many financial variables in particular can only be captured by nonlinear models. The proverbial bubble bursts when it is discovered that efficient nonlinear solution procedures are simply not available.

We referred earlier in this book to "well-known" models. Here is the proper context for that reference. Depending on the form of the nonlinearity and where in the model it occurs, some nonlinear models can be solved in such a way that a true optimal solution results—that is, they are well-behaved. There are a vast number of nonlinear models, however, which are not well-behaved, or cannot be solved efficiently using current knowledge. The only alternative for the model builder in this case is to resort to approaches of a non-optimizing nature. These models will be discussed in the next chapter.

In summary, we can say that although nonlinear formulations of our real-world phenomena are usually more accurate, too many problems are encountered in finding efficient, mathematically tractable solution procedures. Once again, the trade-off between realism and model formulation highlights the fact that successful financial modeling is both an art and a science.

Goal Programming Models

In all the mathematical programming models discussed previously, regardless of the specific nuances which differentiated one from the other, one fact remained. Each approach required that there be only one objective function criterion. This meant that we were either maximizing gross margin or minimizing cost, say, but not both. That is, all these models are characterized by a one-dimensional measure of effectiveness. But in financial management, we know that there could be several measures of effectiveness in a given decision. For example, we might be interested in growth, profitability, and liquidity, to name just a few of the more obvious ones.

The only way we could cope with multiple objectives in the approaches discussed so far is to single out one objective and convert the other objectives into constraining relations. However, this method can seriously affect the usefulness of the results of the model to the financial manager. When we formulate a particular constraint in a model, the solution procedure treats that mathematical statement as binding. If our budget, formulated as a constraint, is $1 million, then the solution mix will be such that it will never be exceeded. The same can be said for all of the other constraints. How realistic is this position?

The financial manager has the discretion in many situations to exceed or fall short of a specified objective (which is not to say that there will be no repercussions of his actions). It was necessary, therefore, to develop models that permitted a multidimensional characterization of the payoff function while at the same time allowing the decision maker, explicitly in the model, to exceed desired or target levels for some of the objectives. The approach that was created to cope with these demands is goal programming modeling.

Key goals identified by the financial manager are formulated as target levels. Any deviation from the target level will incur a "penalty." This "penalty," if it is on the favorable side of the target, might actually be a desirable outcome. On the other hand, a negative deviation is regarded as a true penalty. After all the goals have been identified and evaluated in terms of penalty values, an objective function is developed and expressed in such a way that an optimal solution is generated when a balance is achieved in relation to the goals set forth by the manager. In this way certain goals are exceeded whereas others are not met. The essence of the approach lies in the evaluation of the weights which serve as the penalty values for the objective function.

Goal programming models have excited many model builders who previously were frustrated by the rather stringent requirements of other types of mathematical optimization models. The approach is notable for two main reasons. One, it recognizes explicitly the multidimensional nature of most real-world decisions. Two, it reflects the discretion available to the financial manager in assessing the consequences of exceeding targets or falling short of them. We can look forward to the future when improvements are made to existing goal programming techniques so that more model builders can make effective use of the methodology.

Summary

In this chapter we have presented an overview of optimization methods that have been employed by model builders. After discussing formulation procedures we explained the major types of optimization models based on mathematical programming. The methods used for these models are linear programming, integer programming, nonlinear programming, and goal programming.

Even though these procedures can get very involved, the financial model builder would be remiss to completely exclude any future consideration of them as a potential means for constructing successful models.

5

Simulation in
Financial Modeling

IN this chapter we will discuss the most widely used financial modeling technique—simulation. From our discussion in previous chapters, the reader might be led to believe that, although modeling financial decision situations is appealing, the degree of technical knowledge required by far exceeds what can be expected of the typical financial analyst or manager. This conclusion is not completely correct. The continuum of activities coming under the general term financial modeling is very broad indeed, spanning the entire spectrum from naive or simple approaches to highly sophisticated procedures. Different organizations with differing needs and levels of internal personnel expertise should choose the right approach for their particular purpose. On the other hand, when it comes to optimization models, considerable technical knowledge is indeed required. Perhaps this is the reason why so many financial model builders avoid optimizing models in favor of report generators or simulations. As you will see in this chapter, simulation models offer the model builder a high degree of flexibility.

What Is Simulation?

One of the first ideas that people have when they are first exposed to the concept of simulation is that you do not have to know anything about mathematics in order to use simulation. This impression is not totally correct for several reasons. In the first place, there is no one financial simulation model. Simulation is primarily a methodology. It is a formal procedure for experimenting with a mathematical model for the purpose of better understanding the financial situation that is being modeled. In order to conduct a simulation experiment you must have formulated a model of a particular situation.

Recall our discussion in Chapter 1, where we defined the firm's budget as a mathematical model. The model can be as straightforward as a budget formulation, or it can be an elaborate design of several thousand equations with a vast number of variables. Either way you must have a mathematical model of the system in question.

The existence of the model presupposes all the steps which were discussed in the preceding chapters. Therefore, variable selection, identification of relationships, and parameter estimation are all assumed to have taken place. What then, the reader may ask, is left? In previous chapters, our next step was to solve the model. With simulation, the model is not solved; rather, we perform a series of experiments on the model.

The very feature that made optimization models appealing was their ability to generate an optimal solution to a model. Obviously, if we do not solve a simulation model, then there can be no optimal solution to a simulation model. The fact that we do not worry about solving our model is the major reason why people believe that they do not have to have a mathematical background to use simulation. This is only partially correct. What these same people fail to realize is that a model must still be formulated. To the extent that the formulation phase is straightforward and simple, the technical demands on the model builder are lessened.

Earlier in this chapter we said that simulation is rooted in the notion of experimentation. Experiments are usually characterized by observation and repetition. The model builder observes the effects of different values or states of the variables or assumptions on the outcome measures of the model. The manner in which the experimentation on the model is carried out determines how successful the simulation modeling effort will be from a technical standpoint.

Types of Financial Simulations

In this section we are going to present a number of financial simulation model types ranging from the simple to the sophisticated.

Extended Report Generation

One of the primary responsibilities of the financial groups within an organization is the financial reporting function. The data used in the reporting process, at least in most medium-size and large firms, are gathered and stored on an electronic storage medium. Reporting demands are both periodic and ad hoc. Typically, a specified format is used for each report. The ease with which the reports are generated depends on the way the relevant data items are stored and on the specific computer software capability of the organization.

The reports generated could be geared to a given product, department, or plant or to the entire company. In some cases very elementary arithmetic operations may be required on the data. For example, you might need a report which summarizes sales data across all salespeople in a particular region. As a general rule, reports of this type are mathematically not demanding. The greatest problem in generating them usually is that some data file formats are incompatible. It is rare that the software cannot service the analytical needs of the user in this kind of application.

It did not take long for the financial manager to realize that a very definite need could be met by using the relatively straightforward features of the existing file management software. The reports which supplied budget data and past performance data could take on a new function: they could be used to project operating performance by simply substituting estimated values for some variables and observing the impact on the bottom line. The estimated values could be used as the driving force to observe what alternative scenarios might look like. In this way the financial manager is able to explore various strategies and apprise management of the potential outcomes that could be expected.

In much the same way that sales data are used to trigger a budget, other variables could be tested as to their impact on the operating performance of the company. Many of the values used in this type of analysis are provided after an extensive forecasting program is undertaken by the financial group. The statistical techniques discussed in Chapter 3 can be used to develop reasonable estimates for the trigger variables that form the basis of the experimental computer runs.

There are many individual practitioners in the field of model building who will strenuously object to the inclusion of report generation procedures of this type in a discussion of financial modeling. The reader will observe that we have extended the concept of passive report generation to include an elementary type of experimentation on our "model". The report specification with its additions, subtractions, multiplications, and divisions is our mathematical model. The specific selection of trigger variables chosen by the financial manager serves as a crude type of experiment.

It should be pointed out that a careless or haphazard selection procedure could be costly and confusing. At the very least, the financial manager should select realistic values for the most important target variables. With this approach there is no limit on the number of alternatives that can be investigated. There is one major problem, however. If too many trigger values are allowed to vary at one time, then a combinatorial problem ensues. How can the financial manager expect to understand the cause of the impact on the bottom line if any one of a number of factors could have been responsible? With this type of experimental procedure, the only way to eliminate this problem is to allow only one variable item at a time to vary. As a result of this restriction, the manager could find himself perusing an extremely large number of computer printouts.

In conclusion, it is advisable to explore the potentially useful features of report-generating software packages. As a matter of fact, this approach is the most popular type of "financial modeling" among financial analysts and managers alike. Since there are dozens of vendors providing this kind of software, a careful needs analysis should be conducted. One last caution is in order. The major stumbling block experienced by many financial managers who are using these packages for modeling purposes is that they do not go far enough. After working with the packages for some time, many organizations would like to enhance their modeling efforts so as to incorporate more sophisticated features. They are exasperated to discover that the packages are limited to very elementary analytical operations. Remember, they were designed to be report generators and not financial modeling systems! One should be extremely careful in selecting an approach that can inhibit future modeling enhancement.

Report generators are an excellent place to begin. They fulfill the function of allowing the organization to start slowly, to organize its data bases and get accustomed to learning about financial modeling. Be on guard against locking your organization into limited capability systems. You do not want to find yourself at a dead end. The more sophisticated financial modeling systems have report generation capabilities in addition to a more extensive array of modeling support features. The crucial question the financial manager must answer is whether or not his organization will ever need a full-scale modeling system. If the answer is in the affirmative, then he could begin using a package's report generation features and gradually expand his efforts to include more sophisticated modeling as the need arises. If he is certain that a simple report generator is adequate, then at least careful thought was given to the acquisition decision.

Best-Case/Worst-Case Simulations

The most popular type of deterministic simulation undoubtedly is the now classical approach referred to as best-case/worst-case analysis. The name derives from the practice of selecting two major scenarios to explore during the experimental phase. Instead of randomly selecting values for the key decision variables and running the simulation model with them, the model builder defines a pessimistic scenario and an optimistic scenario. In the former, each variable is assigned the least desirable yet plausible value for purposes of the simulation run (hence the term "pessimistic scenario"). In the optimistic scenario, the most desirable yet plausible values are selected and used for the run.

Using best-case/worst-case analysis gives the decision maker the opportunity to effectively add boundaries to the range of the outcome variables under review. Obviously, the values selected for the input variables under both situations have to be plausible, or else the approach degenerates into a costly exercise in futility. The financial manager can gain a better understanding of the variability of outcomes that can be expected in a given decision situation. While the resulting information is usually not completely satisfactory, it does provide more information than simple report generation.

The approach is usually supplemented by adding the decision maker's most likely estimates for the values of the decision variables. By the way, the implication of a given scenario assumes that all variables, both those under the control of the manager and those out of his control, are set at the designated levels. Therefore, a situation involving a high inflation rate (out of your control) might be combined with a low price (under your control).

Having a simulation run for each of the three scenarios — pessimistic, optimistic, and most likely — enables the decision maker to gauge the relative location, on a continuum, of the outcome variable. Is it closer to the worst case, or is it tending toward the best case? The reader should experience a certain level of discomfort with the last statement. Remember that the manager is usually not in a position to dictate the outcome. He can set levels only for the decision variables under his control. The rest is up to forces and circumstances beyond the control of the manager as decision maker. All a simulation can do for you is to explicitly carry out a given experiment on a well-specified scenario.

Even though best-case/worst-case simulation is entirely based on explicit assumption making, the process of visualizing the effects of decisions has proved to be a very enlightening experience for financial managers. This is especially true if the simulation methodology is augmented by creative use of graphics as the principal means of presenting the results to management.

Although the three-estimate approach is simple and relatively inexpensive, it still has one glaring shortcoming. It does not highlight the individual manager's exposure to risk. Identifying the boundary values merely calibrates the range; it says nothing about the likelihood of their values. More will be said of this fact later in this chapter.

Expected-Value Models

The expected-value model assumes that the average value for each unknown will be used to provide input values for the simulation run. The difficulty arises in the inability to compute an average for some situations for which inadequate data are available. Subjective estimates are substituted by the model builder, and what results is a scenario that resembles the most likely run as described in the previous section.

The other major drawback of the expected-value scenario is that a reliance on past behavior could severely mislead the decision maker. There are a large number of situations for which subjective, future-oriented data are required and, in fact, might be the only appropriate type of data to use in the model.

In summary, although simple and straightforward to use, this approach could cause numerous difficulties for the financial model builder.

Probabilistic Simulation Models

Probabilistic models have as their distinguishing feature the probabilistic characterization of one or more variables. For example, suppose the key variable of interest is sales and we have interviewed the sales manager and obtained the following data:

Sales ($000)	Probability
$1,100	0.25
$1,000	0.50
$ 900	0.25

(It should be mentioned that collecting data of this type may be quite a sensitive matter. The probability distribution may be extracted from the sales manager or statistically estimated from historical data. In the former case, we are dependent on the state of the art of soliciting subjective probability distributions from decision makers. This task should by no means be taken for granted by the model builder.)

Note that in order to construct a probability distribution for a random variable, two items are required: reasonable outcome values and their probabilities of occurrence. The first step is to determine the plausible outcome values of the variable. We recognize that a potentially infinite number of points can be selected. The model builder should limit the selection to as few values as is reasonable in each situation. If this recommendation is not followed, then an unmanageable amount of data would have to be solicited, which could cause a manager to become impatient in the data gathering phase and eventually lose interest in the modeling effort.

Once the outcome values are agreed upon, we must estimate their likelihood of occurence. These probabilities must conform to the properties of probabilities in general. Each must be greater than or equal to zero, and the total of all probabilities must add up to 1. The outcome values must be collectively exhaustive, which means that all the possible outcome measures are identified.

Several approaches have been proposed and used by financial model builders over the years. The choice of a given procedure should depend on its simplicity, managerial acceptance, methodological correctness, and the cost of implementation. The following example may serve as an illustration of what to expect in soliciting subjective probability distributions.

Procedure for Estimating Probabilities

Step 1: Estimate the range over which the variable can assume values.

Step 2: Divide the selected range into a limited number of intervals (equally spaced).

Step 3: Request that the financial manager estimate the relative probabilities of occurrence for each interval.

Step 4: Verify that the probabilities sum to 1 and are in agreement with the beliefs of the financial manager.

It should be quite clear that not all managers will find it an easy task to conscientiously complete the estimation process. The concept of a probability distribution for a future event based on subjective beliefs encounters skepticism from some financial model builders. To help answer these criticisms the model builders should rely on the argument that it is better to have the subjective opinion of the decision maker reflected in the apparatus of the model than to default to the position that, because an event has not occurred, we must assume that all possibilities are equally likely. Remember that we are trying to capture the essence of reality, and this must include, as much as is practically possible, the attitudes of the financial decision maker, for it is he who must live with the consequences of the decision.

So far in this section we have explained the use and estimation of probability distributions for our variables that are treated as probabilistic. A key question that must be asked is, "How many variables in our simulation should be treated as probabilistic?" (Recall that we have a probabilistic simulation if at least one variable is allowed to be probabilistic.) The answer is, as few variables as possible, for reasons of time and cost. This fact will be made abundantly clear later in this chapter.

The reader may wonder why I was so explicit in my explanation of probability distributions. The reason is simple: there is no way to avoid them if you intend to build a probabilistic simulation model. The better the concept is understood by the financial manager, the more likely it is that an intelligent assessment will be made as to which type of simulation model would be the most appropriate in a given situation.

There are several ways to use a probability distribution within a simulation experiment. We have concentrated on the development of subjective probability distributions obtained after an analysis of a given variable was completed. On occasion we may recognize that the probability distribution generated resembles a known standard or theoretical distribution. (Examples of such distributions are normal, exponential, and Poisson distributions.) When this occurs, we simply derive an estimate for the average value and the variance of the probabilistic variable. This information, plus the knowledge of the distribution, can facilitate the actual process of simulating the behavior of the target variable.

Once the model builder has estimated all the values for the deterministic variables and the probability distributions for the random ones, we can begin to design the simulation experiment. There are certain very significant methodological issues that must be considered by the model builder. These concerns are so important that we have devoted an entire chapter to a discussion of them. The next chapter will treat these questions and provide useful guidelines to the financial model builder so that serious errors can be avoided.

The Actual Simulation

The major justification for undertaking the development of a probabilistic simulation model, as opposed to one of the simpler types, is to enable the financial model builder to more effectively portray the exposure to risk inherent in a decision situation. Let us explore this concept further.

The best-case/worst-case simulation model merely establishes the boundary conditions for our measures of effectiveness. For example, if our criterion measure was expected ROI, then all we could state was what the worst conditions would yield and what ROI the best scenario would provide.

Figure 5. Output of a probabilistic simulation model.

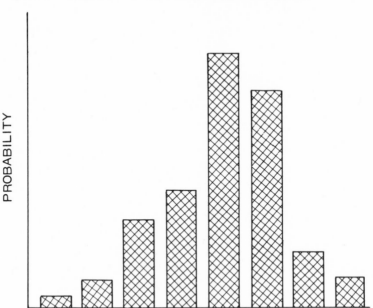

There would never be any indication of what the probability distribution of the expected ROI might look like. Obtaining this probability distribution for our criterion variable(s) is one of the major justifications for engaging in probabilistic modeling. Using probabilistic simulation the financial manager has a visual depiction of the latent risk inherent in the choice situation which is being modeled.

Figure 5 illustrates a plausible probability distribution for the expected ROI which might be obtained from a probabilistic model. Note how much more descriptive the information contained in this figure is than the statement that in the worst case an expected return of −$3 million is expected and in the best possible scenario a return of $5 million is possible. The financial manager can see that although a positive return is very likely, there is still a small chance for a negative return.

A similar outcome distribution can be determined for each of our designated criterion measures. For example, we might also be interested in market share, payback period, revenues, or any other measure of interest to the decision maker. Before getting too excited by the prospect of having this kind of information available, we must remember that this flexibility comes at a price. More on this point later in this and the next chapter.

Having looked at the input and output phases, we are now ready to demonstrate the processing phase of the random simulation model. The key word for this phase is repetition. Repetition is necessary because we must have a sufficiently large sample size in order to be able to generate representative outcome measures. This fact is often ignored by the novice model builder, and the result is usually unfortunate for the manager who must use the information for decision-making purposes.

To illustrate the importance of repetition in simulation, we will use a simple example. Let us assume that our financial model has ten variables. Five of these variables are deterministic (that is, in running the model, their values will be held constant). The remaining five variables are probabilistic and described according to specified probability distributions. For purposes of simplicity we will have only one measure of effectiveness.

Just because we are concentrating at this point on running the model, the reader should not underestimate the task of setting the model objective, identifying the key variables, choosing which ones will be treated as random, and estimating their values and distributions. These steps are integral to the entire modeling effort. Major shortcuts or errors taken at these stages could severely hamper the entire modeling effort. With that caveat in mind, let us continue with the processing phase of our model.

Our next step is to conduct one trial or run of our experiment. This involves setting a value for each of our input variables and then moving through the functional relationships (the equations of our model) one by one until we arrive at a value for our measure of effectiveness. Let us pause for a moment, because it is critical to understand this concept.

Choosing a value for the five deterministic variables is simple, since their values are always going to be the same. The difficulty arises in the selection of values for each of the probabilistic variables. Here is how we do it. For each of these variables we draw a sample value from its range of possible values. We must be certain that the manner in which the value is selected is governed by the specified probability distribution. In other words, after a large number of values for each variable are extracted, their frequencies should be patterned after the specified distribution. The more trials we run of our model, the closer the pattern should be to the underlying specified distribution. If too few observations are obtained, then the pattern might not reflect what the decision maker believed the distribution to be. The effect of this would be an inaccurate picture of the impact of the variables on the measure of effectiveness.

After the first trial or run of the model we record the value for the measure of effectiveness. It is now time for the second trial. A new set of sample values for the five probabilistic variables is generated and combined with the constant values for the deterministic variables. A new outcome measure results and is also recorded. Because our second set of sample values is likely to be different from our first set, we can expect a different value for the outcome measure. In general, each trial can be expected to have a different mix of input values for the variables, and this should result in a different value for the outcome measure.

We continue these iterations or trials until a decision is made to stop the simulation. The decision process will be explained in the next chapter. Once the trials have ceased we must use the information about the outcome measure obtained from each run and construct a probability function for it. This function is based on the frequency with which each value occurred in the course of the simulation experiment. Refer again to Figure 5 in this chapter.

In our illustrative example we had only ten variables, of which only five were singled out and treated probabilistically. We can have as many probabilistic variables as the financial model builder feels are necessary in order to capture the essence of reality. However, the more variables we have, the more complex our model becomes in all stages ranging from model formulation all the way to model implementation.

Summary

In this chapter we have described simulation models. We differentiated descriptive simulation models from optimization models, which are normative in approach. The remainder of the chapter was devoted to an explanation of four classes of simulation models: extended report generators, best-case/worst-case analysis, expected-value models, and probabilistic or risk-analysis models.

In the next chapter we will focus on some of the more important methodological considerations inherent in building financial simulation models.

6

Some Operational Issues
in Building
Simulation Models

FROM the discussion in the previous chapter the reader is likely to conclude that random simulation models, because of their technical requirements, are not an integral component of all packages. This conclusion is correct. Many of the vendors supplying report generator packages have limited their markets to firms that only desire to format and reformat management reports. Although the data-handling capabilities of some of the more complete systems are quite extensive, true modeling efforts can be thwarted by the lack of efficient means to change key account information, substitute computed forecasts, and permit repeated trials.

Financial model building is not just mathematics but rather an integrated support effort that facilitates a productive climate for data collection, analysis, and implementation of model results. A modeling system that is hard to use or cumbersome will rarely be used properly by the financial manager, if it ever gets used at all. For example, trying to take a package designed for file management and reporting and forcing it to perform in a mode for which it was not intended can be counterproductive or downright harmful to the modeling effort of an organization.

True simulation capability necessitates, in my opinion, support for both deterministic and probabilistic simulation models. Obviously, the former is simpler than the latter to develop, and that is one of the principal reasons for its popularity. One should be extremely careful to scrutinize the vendor's documentation for signs that it can support probabilistic simulation models. Some other terms used synonymously are risk model, risk analysis, random model, and Monte Carlo analysis.

Probabilistic simulation can also be implemented in inhouse models which are custom-designed and do not use standard financial modeling systems. However the capability is achieved, the financial model builder will find it an important addition to his repertoire. Even with the difficulties of estimating probability distributions, and despite potentially expensive run costs, there are situations when anything less than probabilistic simulation can cause major hurdles in closing the judgmental gap. The model builder, in conjunction with the financial manager, should assess the benefits and costs of employing a risk-analysis model formulation. Some managers, because of their style and receptivity to modeling, will find it more appealing and potentially more useful than others. In this kind of environment, the likelihood of overcoming some of the previously identified obstacles is markedly improved.

There is still another avenue to get to the eventual use of probabilistic models. That path is through planned evolutionary growth. If a system supported both deterministic and probabilistic simulation approaches, then one would start out building deterministic models. Any model so developed could be designed with the idea that some key variables will eventually be treated as probabilistic. This flexibility can go a long way toward reducing the costs of model modification. Once the financial manager expresses a desire for more realism or a better understanding of the exposure to risk, the model builder can gradually introduce probabilistic components where appropriate.

It is always preferable to get managers involved with simpler modeling experiences so that they can grow in their knowledge of modeling as they become more familiar with and accustomed to the benefits that can be derived from a well thought-out program. Of course, there is a flip side to this argument. If the financial manager is ready to grow with the modeling experience but the model does not have the capacity for growth, then you can expect a certain degree of resentment or frustration. The person who will have to "take the heat" is the model builder. Therefore, it will behoove the manager who is just getting started in financial modeling to give serious consideration to whether or not probabilistic simulation capability should be in the system specifications. I think it should. The eventual decision is yours.

Choosing a Simulation Language

In this section we will focus on the choice of a language for a financial simulation model. In reality, the model builder does not always consider this choice explicitly. Often, the decision is made when an organization adopts a vendor's financial modeling system. Nevertheless, no discussion of this subject would be complete without an overview of the types of simulation languages available.

In order to be processed by a computer, instructions must be coded in a language that is understood by the host machine. This language is very cumbersome and impossible for most people to comprehend, let alone use. Therefore, higher-level languages are developed so that programmers can communicate with the computer without knowing the host language. The programmer's instructions are then automatically translated into the machine's "native" language.

The financial model builder constructs a simulation model which is programmed to be run on the computer. The central issue in the choice of a language is how much "programming" should be done by the financial analyst or manager. The entire spectrum of effort expected by the model builder is incorporated in today's modeling software. We will try to unravel, for the reader, the current state of affairs.

Several programming languages were developed in the late 1950s and early 1960s to support engineering or statistical applications. The most widely known of these languages are FORTRAN and ALGOL. Eventually, the modeling groups in organizations began to develop financial models using these languages, which were readily available and known to model builders. At the time financial modeling systems had not been developed. With the advent of time-sharing, two conversational languages became popular with model-building groups. These languages are BASIC and APL. APL in particular has some very attractive features that have drawn special attention from model builders in all disciplines.

With interest in modeling spreading throughout organizations, it became apparent to many practitioners that their efforts were being hindered by the requirement that the user must be a programmer in order to use these languages. To satisfy this market need, several special-purpose simulation languages were developed. These languages, notably SIMSCRIPT and GPSS, performed much of the housekeeping chores required in simulation modeling. As a rule, these higher-level languages were based on some of the lower-level ones. They served as an interface between the model builder and the computer language. Once a flowchart of the model logic is developed, the model builder selects the appropriate instructions to perform the indicated operations. Today these modeling languages are widely used throughout the world and have greatly helped facilitate the growth of simulation modeling.

It should be pointed out that all of the languages described in this section have the capability to support both deterministic and probabilistic modeling.

For many technically trained individuals all of the previously described languages cause no problems in building models. Surprisingly, many financial analysts have labored successfully in developing applications of financial modeling using FORTRAN, BASIC, and SIMSCRIPT among other languages. There is, however, a very serious drawback which must be mentioned. The typical financial manager is not willing or able to get mired in the technical details of a programming language. Designers of software must develop languages that accept terms and commands which are either familiar to the financial analyst or manager or easily learned. These command languages form the nucleus of the many financial modeling systems on the market today. Vendors have responded to the requirements of the nontechnical user and have provided a wide-ranging choice of options to satisfy virtually every modeling need of the financial manager. Later chapters will discuss some of the caveats in choosing a vendor.

The reader with knowledge of some of the languages mentioned in this section would probably recognize some of their conventions peering through the commands of the financial modeling systems. This is the case because many of the packages are APL-based, FORTRAN-based, and so forth. This does not mean, however, that they are difficult to use. On the contrary, some packages were designed to obviate the need for any type of computer programmer support. These highly conversational systems were meant to be used by the manager with no technical background. Within a relatively short period of time, all financial modeling systems can be expected to evolve into this type. It cannot happen soon enough. In all probability, the existence of easy-to-use software will accelerate the growth of financial model building in organizations.

Regardless of the specific language or modeling system adopted by an organization, much thought must still be given to the manner in which a simulation model is developed. One of the most critical factors in probabilistic modeling is the approach taken to selecting values for the random variables at each trial. The next section is devoted to a discussion of this topic.

Selecting Random Values

In this section we will explain one of the most pivotal concepts in probabilistic modeling: that of generating values for the variables in each trial. Remember that each of the variables in the model is either deterministic or probabilistic. In the case of a deterministic variable, its value will always be the same. However, when it comes to probabilistic variables we must rely on the underlying probability distribution as a basis for value selection.

We can illustrate the concept of probabilistic value selection pictorially as in Figure 6, which displays the three possible outcomes for sales along with their associated probability values. Instead of a tabular format we have chosen to represent the information in the form of a pie chart.

Using data from a previous example, we can now select a value for our variable. The area devoted to the specific outcomes in the pie chart is proportional to their probabilities of occurrence in the real world as gleaned from the investigative phase of the modeling project. All that is needed is a procedure to extract a given value for each trial of our simulation experiment. This selection procedure must be random so that values occur in proportion to their likelihood of occurrence in the real situation. Figure 7 illustrates a device which, when spun, will

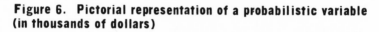

Figure 6. Pictorial representation of a probabilistic variable (in thousands of dollars)

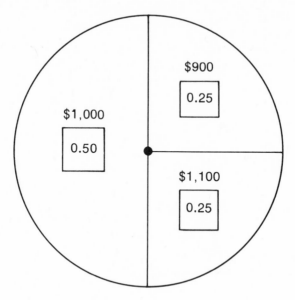

select one of the three possible values. If our spinner control is random, we have a bona fide procedure for selecting values purely according to their probabilities.

Obviously, we have been explaining the conceptual process and not the actual method of selection followed in a computer simulation. The actual procedure is based on the principles of random number generation. Any probabilistic simulation model developed must address this task of random value selection. General-purpose languages like FORTRAN and BASIC treat the function at the subroutine level and then tailor the function to a particular theoretical or empirical distribution. The resulting procedure usually entails the creation of several lines of computer code for each probabilistic variable being simulated. In the case of special-purpose simulation languages, random number generators for some of the most

Figure 7. Random value selection.

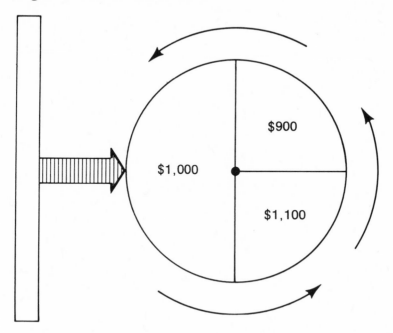

common distributions are preprogrammed. Most of the financial modeling packages that support probabilistic simulations treat the function in a manner similar to that used by the special-purpose simulation languages. In these applications the hardest part of the process is the establishment of the probability distributions for the variables. The actual generation process is usually handled without any serious difficulty, particularly in some of the more conversational financial modeling packages.

Regardless of the type of implementation mode that is adopted for random value selection, the model builder is still responsible for data gathering, model development, and interpretation of the results. The fact that it is simple to generate a probabilistic phenomenon does not mean that it is required

Figure 8. Sales distribution.

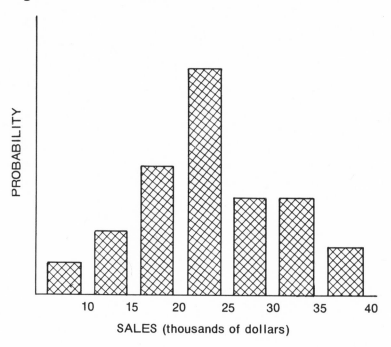

for model accuracy or even that it is cost-effective. In fact, in some cases a great deal of ingenuity is required of the model builder in order to capture many of the nuances of the real-world situation under investigation. We will illustrate this with the notion of conditional dependence of probabilistic variables.

Suppose we need estimates of sales for two years in a new-product-planning model. Since our model is future-oriented, we have to rely on the subjective distribution as extracted from the product manager. After careful analysis we might come up with the probability distribution for sales as given in Figure 8.

The key question that should be asked about this distribution is what it describes: first-year sales? second-year sales? or cumulative sales? If we assume that it is for both first- and second-year sales, we can raise the legitimate objection that once first-year sales are known, we should revise our estimates for the second year accordingly. In other words, second-year sales are conditional on the performance of the sales in the first year. To model this process accurately, the financial model builder will have to develop a scheme capable of representing the multistage nature of the decision problem.

A plausible approach would be to generate a sales estimate for the first year according to the distribution presented in Figure 8. However, to generate an estimate for the second year, we will have to create two or more conditional distributions reflecting the scenario that occurred in year one. For example, one distribution might be based on poor first-year sales, another on mediocre sales, and a third on a banner first-year's sales performance. In this way we have introduced more realism, but at the expense of a multilevel random-value generation procedure.

More work has to be done by designers of financial model packages so that complex phenomena can be modeled without involving the financial manager in excessive model-logic details.

In this section we have presented the essence of the procedure for generating values for random variables in a probabilistic simulation model. Hopefully, the reader has a better understanding of the magnitude of the effort required to undertake the development of simulation models of this type. In some situations the benefits are worth more than the sacrifices incurred.

When to Stop a Simulation Experiment

In this section of the chapter we focus our attention on one of the most troublesome aspects of the simulation experiment.

Researchers have spent many years attempting to obtain a definitive procedure for determining the optimum sample size for an experimental simulation. The recommendations are typically phrased in statistical terminology and, as a result, are ignored by most practitioners. The core of the dilemma is the trade-off between the precision of the estimates and the cost of additional computer trials.

It is rare that the documentation of financial modeling systems contains an explicit, thorough discussion of run size. Often a recommendation is offered to run a model 1,000 times. It is assumed that the estimate is conservative and any results achieved would be accurate. The advice given by technical support personnel is of a similar kind. Since the financial manager is exposed to this rather casual approach to the determination of run size, it is not surprising that he does not take the problem as seriously as he should. The net effect is that all that is considered is the increasing computer charges being accumulated, particularly when the simulation model is being run on the computer of an outside service bureau.

Under these circumstances it is not surprising to see model builders cutting short simulation runs before adequate conclusions can be reached from the available output. The reader must appreciate the fact that the user has no explicit sign that the model should be continued. Since it is an experiment, the decision as to the number of trials is under the control of the financial model builder. This decision is often made before the first run when the analyst is asked how many trials are to be processed by the computer.

We are arguing in this book for a more intelligent assessment of the sample size required in a financial simulation model. Perhaps the only way this idea can be fostered is to equip the technical support staff with the expertise to help the first-time user of a financial model in this decision. Opponents of this position argue that the support specialist's plea for adequate run size is usually ignored by the novice model builder on the grounds that it is merely an excuse to sell more computer time.

My inclusion of this topic in the book is an attempt to alert both sides of the controversy that there is merit in both positions. The resolution of the matter lies in the establishment of a relationship of trust between the financial model builder and the financial manager. Once a level of confidence and mutual respect is reached, we can concentrate on developing a useful model for the organization.

The Need for Simulation-Model Validation

The ultimate measure of the worth of any simulation model is its ability to help the financial manager make better decisions. So much can change in the environment to cause even a good decision to lead to an undesirable outcome that it behooves the model builder to be sure that the financial model is valid.

The validity of a model cannot be ascertained without a clear statement of why the model was developed in the first place. Validation implies the existence of a purpose. Once the purpose is known, we must verify that the simulation model does indeed capture the essence of the situation being modeled. This, of course, is much easier to achieve if we're describing a real present situation. A more difficult problem exists when the simulation model depicts a hypothetical future situation. In that case much greater emphasis must be given to ensuring that the logic modules of the simulation accurately reflect the views of the financial manager. Both the model logic and the underlying assumptions must be subjected to meticulous scrutiny. The greater the degree of confidence in the dimensions of the model and in the modeling process itself, the closer the organization is to validating the model.

There are certain measures which could be verified statistically when and if the simulation model is tested on the past. We can achieve this kind of model calibration by defining a base case that is predicated on the past behavior of the process being modeled. Once enough confidence in the financial model is obtained, it can be used by the financial manager in support of his decision-making effort. In situations where new information becomes available, the model can be updated to reflect any estimates or relationships which might have changed.

If should be pointed out that model validation can be a very subjective thing. Even if the model builder presents a virtually unlimited amount of documentation in support of the validity of the model, it might still not be enough to convince the manager who must use it. In this case the model builder has failed. The failure is one of communication. Whenever the manager refuses to accept a tool which was purportedly developed with his support, the blame must be laid on the model builder. If the financial manager was truly involved in the process of modeling, there should be no surprises at the implementation stage. Any fears that surfaced should have been allayed. The model is an extension of the manager, and it should be acceptable to him if it is ever to be used in the front line of decision making. Once again, strong communications skills are a most important asset for a successful financial model builder.

In conclusion, there is no easy and precise way to guarantee the validity of a simulation model. What exists is a series of processes which can be followed to increase the level of validity of a model. The ultimate perspective, 20/20 hindsight, is just not available to us when we need it.

Conclusion

In this last section of the chapter on operational issues of simulation modeling, our intent is to offer a perspective on how the financial model builder should approach simulation modeling.

Regardless of the manner of implementing simulation modeling, the concerns presented in this chapter will have to be addressed. Simulation is a methodology with enormous potential—for success as well as for failure. As systems are developed that can be used by more and more managers, often with little or no technical background, it becomes all the more important to confront the methodological questions raised in this chapter, or the future of financial modeling will be in doubt. When a model fails to help a manager in the decision-making process, all of modeling suffers a setback. The particular reasons for the failure are rarely identified; we only hear that financial modeling does not work!

Because of its apparent simplicity, simulation is the technique most prone to abuse. It has been referred to by some as merely a game. This position is bolstered by the central role "Monte Carlo" analysis plays in probabilistic simulation modeling. Both the manager and the analyst must be prepared to counter these accusations. The very nature of a simulation experiment contributes to this criticism. Only by careful model building that makes explicit all assumptions can we convince the financial manager that the effects of future decisions can be anticipated and explored through the use of simulation modeling. This convincing will not be accomplished through words. The eventual deciding factor will be the results obtained in the financial departments of organizations. Financial managers using financial models successfully will be the best selling agents. It is imperative that the financial model builder prove himself under fire—the arena where real decisions are made.

7

Sensitivity Analysis in Financial Modeling

NO book on financial modeling, especially an introductory one, would be complete without a presentation and discussion of sensitivity analysis. As a matter of fact, the process of modeling demands that some type of sensitivity analysis be performed on the model.

Sensitivity analysis and its proper context were defined by Robert Blanning as follows:

> The central concept of management science is the concept of a model—that is, a relationship between those variables under the control of a decision maker (decision variables), those not under his control (environmental variables), and one or more measures of cost or performance. To solve a model means to (1) experiment with the model to calculate the anticipated cost and performance of proposal decisions (simulation) or to calculate the decision variables that minimize or maximize a single measure of cost or perform-

Figure 9. Probing the model through sensitivity analysis.

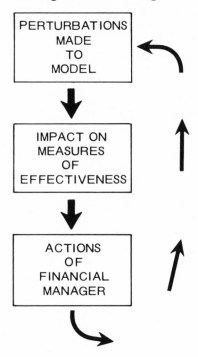

ance with constraints on other measures (optimization), and (2) to perform sensitivity analyses that measure the rate of change of the "output" of the model (the cost and performance measures) with respect to the "inputs" (the decisions and the environment).*

The financial model builder, in attempting to obtain a better understanding of the decision situation, probes the solution space so as to gain additional insight beyond the mere solution of the model. Figure 9 illustrates the nature of the probing

*"The Sources and Uses of Sensitivity Information," *Interfaces,* August 1974, p. 32.

process and how it eventually affects managerial decisions. This iterative process continues until the financial manager has reached a level of understanding that would support making a decision.

The real insight to be gained from the modeling effort typically comes about during this stage of analysis. L. Dan Maxim and Frank Cook have dubbed this stage of financial model building "intellectual post processing," or IP^2.* They argue that all too often insufficient time and effort are allocated to assimilation of the model's solution. Proper project planning and control are essential features that cannot be ignored if an organization wants to mount a successful financial modeling program. The insight gained from sensitivity analysis provides an excellent vehicle for the financial manager to help close the judgmental gap between model results and the real world.

Sensitivity Analysis in Optimization Models

In Chapter 4 we have examined the essential components of an optimization model— its "objective function" and constraining relationships, usually in the form of inequalities or equations. In this section we will present some of the aspects of optimization models that can be probed through sensitivity analysis. There are five of them:

1. Objective function coefficients.
2. Technological coefficients.
3. Maximum or minimum resource limits.
4. Adding or deleting a constraining resource.
5. Adding or deleting a decision variable.

Financial Risk Analysis, New York: AMACOM, 1972, p.49.

Each of these concerns of sensitivity analysis will be discussed in some detail.

Probing Objective Function Coefficients

Recall that the objective function represents the mathematical statement of the criterion measure for the model (for example, maximize profit or minimize cost). The original values used in the model's objective function were the best estimates available at the time. Since they are only estimates, we could have made an error, particularly if our model is of a future planned process. As standard procedure, sensitivity analysis is applied in this area to investigate the ranges of the coefficients, particularly percentage differences above end below the targeted value. By observing the effects of these coefficient changes on the output measures of the model, we obtain a better understanding of the dynamics of the model. In other words, we shift our focus from a one-value orientation to an incremental-change orientation. The latter approach is more comfortably received by financial analysts and managers alike. Figure 10 depicts a plausible result of probing the impact of one variable's coefficients on the value of the objective function.

We could perform this type of analysis on each of the critical decision variables. We might discover that a particular coefficient is extremely sensitive and that greater care should be given the estimation of its value. This is a good example of how the financial model can shed light on the workings of a particular decision situation—one of the desirable properties of a good model which was discussed in Chapter 1.

Probing Technological Coefficients

The function of technological coefficients is to relate the decision variables to the maximum or minimum resource limi-

Figure 10. Graph of change impact of an objective function coefficient.

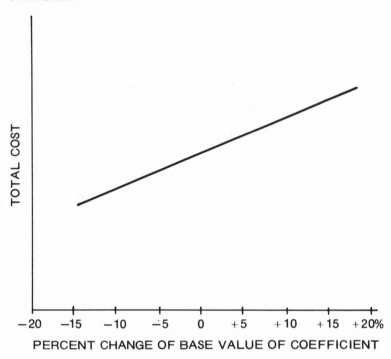

PERCENT CHANGE OF BASE VALUE OF COEFFICIENT

tations. For example, given a certain upper dollar limit on capital expansion, we would be interested in each project's rate of resource utilization. Suppose five projects are available to the decision maker for possible investment with the following estimated costs:

Project A	$ 5,000
Project B	$10,000
Project C	$20,000
Project D	$18,000
Project E	$ 8,750

Unfortunately, the budget limitation for all investments is set at $35,000. The decision is to choose among the five alternatives such that the total budget is not exceeded. The specific project costs, in this example, represent technological coefficients.

In the case of a machine, technological coefficients would measure the impact of improvements in technology on the productivity of capital. In the case of financial securities, it would be represented by the respective contribution to the target level of return.

For example, the return on common stocks might be estimated at 10 percent, bonds at 8 percent, and commodities at 9 percent. Each of these estimates would represent the technological coefficients of the respective financial investment vehicle. It is easy to see why a financial manager would be interested in exploring the impact of changes in the technological coefficients. The insight gained from this analysis could prove beneficial in the decision to reallocate the firm's resources to achieve more favorable results.

The proposal to replace a printing press with a more modern one could be analyzed using sensitivity analysis by substituting its coefficient values for those of the existing press. The outcome from this substitution, in conjunction with more traditional forms of analysis, will provide added information on which the financial manager can base a decision or recommendation. Another area where this application can prove useful is in man/machine trade-off situations. Both can be modeled and the technological implications of each option reviewed.

Caution is advised in this area of sensitivity analysis, because the values subjected to sensitivity analysis are coefficients of decision variables as they appear in the resource constraint relationships. Any insights gained by the manager are directly related to the quality of the estimation process. It is of little value to do extensive analysis on data of little integrity. Misplaced analysis has contributed to the demise of many budding modeling efforts.

Probing Maximum or Minimum Resource Limits

In this application, sensitivity analysis focuses on the values designated as the upper or lower limits of our specified resources. Some examples of these resources are market share, budget level, working capital requirements, and manpower restrictions. In the course of identifying variables and estimating parameters, the model builder identified the resources that were critical to the financial decision situation and estimated their availability levels. Once the optimization model is solved, the financial manager might be interested in exploring the impact of loosening or tightening the specified levels of the resources.

For example, what would be the impact on profitability if we modified the working capital requirement? Several plausible values could be tried to enable the financial manager to better comprehend the nature and impact of this particular resource constraint. Similarly, a merger or acquisition and its concomitant influx of cash could be explored by means of a sensitivity analysis of the cash constraint or any other restriction.

Analyzing the Effect of Adding or Deleting a Constraining Resource

This aspect of sensitivity analysis explores the impact on the objective function of changing the structural relationships of the original model rather than modifying just a single value. The idea of model modification is a basic one in financial modeling. Managers frequently recognize that a particular constraint was mistakenly omitted in the original formulation or that a constraint that was originally considered relevant is in fact unimportant. For whatever reason, the basic model is often changed, and it is usually impossible in a reasonably complex model to ascertain the immediate impact of such changes on the objective function.

This type of sensitivity analysis raises an additional problem. Each time we add another constraint we add to the computational burden, which has a direct impact on the costs incurred in running the model. If the cost/benefit trade-off is ignored, we might find ourselves in the situation where we continually expand the size of the model in a search for greater realism. Unfortunately, a larger model is not necessarily a better model. The objective should be to develop the simplest model possible that captures the essence of the situation being modeled. There are many variables and relationships that are present in the real-world situation but are extraneous to the financial decision. Without a carefully thought-out plan, the financial model builder could easily allow this activity to degenerate into a time-consuming and costly exercise without any tangible benefits.

Analyzing the Effect of Adding or Deleting a Decision Variable

The principal characteristic of this type of sensitivity analysis is that it affords the financial manager an opportunity to explore additions or deletions to the firm's product line. In a capital-budgeting context it focuses on the addition or deletion of an additional capital project. As in the previous case, we are modifying the structural model of our system and not simply changing a single coefficient.

The number of options available to the financial manager

are virtually limitless when it comes to exploring additions to the list of decision variables (for example, new products or projects). Only those situations that are plausible should be investigated by the model builder.

· There are some good reasons why it is advantageous to restrict changes to the variable structure of a model. For each variable added we must consider whether or not it creates a need for another constraining relationship. We must also estimate a coefficient for the decision variable that appears in the objective function. After identifying each constraining relation in which the new variable appears, we must estimate the coefficients of the decision variable in each of these equations. As this should have made clear, an apparently simple decision to add a new decision variable to a model has serious ramifications. In the case of a variable being deleted from the model we merely reverse the procedure. For example, for each deleted variable we must refer to all constraints in which that variable appears and remove it from the relationship. It is quite possible that the deleted variable is the only one present in the constraint. The effect is, therefore, to delete the constraint.

The reader should now possess a good understanding of the types of sensitivity analysis that can be performed on an optimization model. We can add an explicit classification scheme to the five procedures described:

- *Value analysis* — in this case our attention is limited to the change of one variable or value in a model.
- *Range analysis* — in this case we are interested in the relevant ranges for all coefficients or values for which the optimum levels for the decision variables are valid. In other words, how much can the value change before it is no longer optimum?
- *Parameterization* — this involves requesting a given coefficient or value to vary over a predetermined range.

The input value is then compared with the outcome measure for each value over the designated range.

A reading of the five applications discussed earlier in the chapter will uncover the presence of these three classes of sensitivity analysis.

There is a major consideration relevant to the use of sensitivity analysis in all areas of model building, but particularly when dealing with optimization models. This is the concept of change control. If the model builder attempts to change too many factors simultaneously, the precise impact of each input factor on the outcome measure is impossible to determine. Because of an understandable desire to save computer time and costs there might be a tendency to try to change too much at one time. The net result is often zero insight. The model builder should always budget adequate time and money so that a proper effort is devoted to the sensitivity analysis phase of a project.

Costs can be effectively controlled in an optimization environment because a great deal of the sensitivity analysis on the model can be accomplished by using the original model solution as a starting point. It is not necessary to return to the proverbial "step one" each time the financial manager poses a new question. This capability is a direct result of the type of model and the power of many of the production optimization software packages that are available for use by the model builder. We will see in the next section that this is not the case with financial simulation models.

Sensitivity Analysis in Simulation Models

In earlier chapters we described simulation modeling and its potential as a tool for financial modeling. Perhaps its greatest benefits are derived after sensitivity analyses are performed on the original model. This is because of the experimental nature of the procedure. However, there is one major problem in using sensitivity analysis with a simulation model. In a simulation we are required to rerun the entire model each time we wish to investigate a change in one of the variables or relationships. This, it will be recalled, is not the case with optimization models.

Coping with Uncertainty in Deterministic Simulations

In our discussion of deterministic models, we said that they were the most widely used financial models. The best way for financial managers to cope with uncertainty when employing a deterministic simulation model is to make extensive use of sensitivity analysis. By varying input conditions or structural relationships the manager can explore the sensitivity of the outcome measure(s) to these perturbations. Alternative scenarios can be explored at any desired level of variety or detail. As a matter of fact, if sensitivity analysis is not used in a deterministic simulation experiment, there is a serious ques-. tion as to the utility of the entire effort.

The model builder can explore errors in parameter estimation or the exact form of the structural relationship among variables. Without sensitivity analysis it would take a Herculean modeling effort to truly capture the decision situation along with the inherent dimensions of risk. Most financial managers use careful changes to the model as the principal vehicle for exploring the "risk map" surrounding a particular decision.

Interactive Modeling and Sensitivity Analysis

"Conversational" or interactive simulation models open up a whole new area for financial managers who wish to exploit the benefits of sensitivity analysis. The first of these benefits is the use of "what if" modeling. The manager is able to communicate with the model in a direct, immediate way, which capitalizes on and stimulates the creative process. As the results of one question are explored and reported to the financial manager, he can react by posing other questions. It is difficult to overestimate the benefits interactive modeling has brought to the financial modeling programs of many organizations. Elsewhere in this book we have stated that interactive modeling should be looked at very carefully and possibly made a design requirement for the company that is just getting started in financial modeling.

Still on the subject of design requirements, one should insist that the "what if" capability be implemented in a user-oriented manner. Many developers insist that their models have a "what if" capability. I liken the statement to that of a salesman of television sets who insists that a 100-pound television set is "portable." The presence of the "what if" feature is not enough. It must be easy to use and conserve resources as much as possible. If it is properly designed and used, the financial manager can grasp the dynamics of a situation and gain valuable insights into the riskiness of a decision.

A second major benefit of interactive modeling is the feature referred to as either "goal seeking" or "backward analysis." The concept is quite simple. Often a financial manager will have an idea of a target level or goal for an output measure. What he wants to know is the level of the input factors that is required to achieve the desired level of the outcome measure. The simulation model uses a reverse calculation procedure to derive the appropriate input values.

The financial manager can use goal seeking to explore the feasibility of pursuing several different combinations of decision variables each of which, according to the model, would achieve the desired outcome. Goal seeking is a relatively new feature of some financial modeling packages, and it will be some time before its overall usefulness to the financial model builder can be assessed. In my own experience, neither support analysts nor managers know how to use the technique to best advantage.

In summary, we can safely say that interactive modeling is going to become even more widespread as modelers and managers learn of the benefits to be derived from this approach. This fact is well recognized by external vendors of financial modeling software. Too many in-house modeling groups have not yet recognized the real advantages to be achieved from interactive modeling in all stages of the modeling process.

Sensitivity Analysis in Probabilistic Simulations

All of our discussion relating to deterministic modeling is applicable to probabilistic simulations as well. The major extension is the requirement to explore the impact of the underlying probability distributions. That is, we must determine the effects of changes to the probability distributions of key variables. When one considers that many of these distributions are based on subjective estimates, it becomes even more important to investigate the impact of mis-estimation on the outcome measure(s) of the model.

One of the more obvious consequences of probabilistic simulation is an increase in model complexity. This is the price we pay for increased model realism. The combinatorial nature of the model further complicates the testing phase and the sensitivity analysis phase. This complexity is reflected in the increased costs of running these models. In fact, this argument is advanced by many potential users who say that the costs of running a probabilistic model would be prohibitive and who therefore decide to develop deterministic models and to run extensive sensitivity analyses studies on their model. Proponents of some of the more sophisticated financial modeling systems argue that only a risk-analysis model can capture the nature of real financial decisions. Perhaps, as financial model users outgrow their deterministic model's limited capabilities, we will see an increase in the use of probabilistic models.

Sensitivity Analysis and its Impact on Multidimensional Objectives

One of the most obvious recent trends in model building has been to rely more and more on formulating models that have multiple objective functions. The manager typically deals with situations which simply cannot be adequately modeled using a single objective. Hence, there is a real need to identify all outcome measures relevant for a given financial decision.

The sheer magnitude of the complexity in dealing with several dimensions is a challenge to the financial model builder. For example, suppose a company has a pre-tax profit target of 20 percent, a sales growth target of 15 percent, and a manpower growth target of 2 percent. In this case one objective might be attained only at the expense of one or more of the other objectives. It is virtually impossible to understand the manifold interrelationships between the objectives of the model without a carefully designed program of sensitivity analysis. In this type of situation the objectives are usually conflicting. The nature and extent of their impact must be first identified in order for the effects of the objectives to be understood. Sensitivity analysis, in this context, enables the financial manager to cope in a more insightful way with the complexity of the situation. Recognizing the fact that complete certainty is an unreachable goal, we must strive to reduce the uncertainty to a level that is acceptable to the financial manager, given the trade-offs between time, costs, and resources.

Use of Graphics Output

One of the most exciting hardware developments to come along in recent years is the new generation of graphic terminals. Innovations have taken place in both hard-copy and visual display terminals.

Simulation modeling is notorious for the amount of printed output it generates, due to the large number of trials that are typically run in an experiment. Such proliferation of printed output can easily lead to information overload, which typically results in a tendency not to look at anything. Whereas excessive data in tabular form are difficult to assimilate, graphic output enables the financial model builder to capture the dynamics of the data in a simple pictorial form. Recent improvements permit the overlap of several relationships on one graph, which further aids in detecting the interrelationships inherent in the system without time-consuming scanning of tabular data. Pictorial representation has more eye appeal and is easier to remember and understand. These two characteristics facilitate in a subtle way the acceptance of the model by management.

An improvement of a more startling nature is the introduction of multicolored output on visual display screens. The financial analyst is now able to observe the behavior of several variables in a simulation model simultaneously on a video display screen. The visual impact is indeed impressive! A creative model builder can think of innovative and effective ways to present the output of a sensitivity analysis to management in ways that programmers of years past hadn't even dreamed of.

Clearly, as with many innovations in this field, there is a danger of creating a situation where there is more show than substance. Nonetheless, as long as you keep on your guard in implementing a graphics application, you can be certain that the technology will be a very effective asset in marketing the modeling program to your organization's financial managers.

Summary

In this chapter we have discussed the pivotal role of sensitivity analysis in financial modeling. The five aspects of optimization models that can profit from sensitivity analysis are (1) objective function coefficients, (2) technological coefficients, (3) maximum or minimum resource limits, (4) adding or deleting a constraining resource, and (5) adding or deleting a decision variable. A distinction was made between value analysis, range analysis, and parameterization as they apply to the general problem of probing the solution space of a model.

In our discussion of sensitivity analysis in simulation modeling, we looked at the issue of coping with uncertainty in deterministic models and interactive or conversational modeling. With respect to the latter we focused on "what if" analysis and "goal seeking" or "backward analysis."

Our discussion of sensitivity analysis was extended to probabilistic simulation models, problems with multiple objectives, and finally the enormous potential of graphic output for model results.

8

Organizational Issues in Financial Modeling

THE organizational placement of the financial modeling effort depends to a great extent on the size of the organization and its previous experience with modeling in general.

Companies that have been extensively engaged in building models often have a special department, sometimes associated with the data processing group. Initial efforts at modeling in this type of environment would necessitate requesting an analyst to work with the financial group. The advantage to the approach is that it is possible to have a trained, experienced model builder who can call on his peers if there is a technical question that must be resolved. A key assumption is that the analyst is competent in the technical matter as well as a good communicator who can handle the interpersonal dimensions of the assignment.

The informal organizational grapevine provides a sensitive barometer for the potential success or failure of the financial model undertaking. Word spreads fast within an organization on the perceived competence of the modeling group. If the financial manager hears horror stories from other managers about the past efforts of the modeling group, you can be certain that he will consider other alternatives before relying on the designated internal expertise. On the other hand, if the financial manager receives positive feedback from his peers regarding cost-effective implementations of models in their respective areas, a more conducive atmosphere for a productive association exists. I do not see anything wrong with judging the performance of a modeling group on its past achievements (or lack of same) within an organization. When you consider the perspective of the decision maker who is devoting his department's resources and risking his own reputation, enough care cannot be taken to ensure that the partners in the effort have respect for each other's competence.

The other alternative which is frequently followed, especially among smaller organizations that do not have an internal modeling group, is to develop the capability in a member of the financial group. As we have seen, a financial model can range anywhere from a report generator to an extensive model utilizing econometric techniques. It is important to consider the demands that the development of the modeling effort will place on the firm.

For example, if the extent of the modeling activity is merely to reformat data that exist on computer files in order to generate a budget, profit-and-loss statement, or balance sheet, then extensive training and resources are typically not required. Although this situation usually does not create a substantial amount of organizational friction, some problems could arise if the data are not under the direct control of the department. The data processing group could get a bit testy when "an outsider" is allowed to manipulate files for whose maintenance it is responsible.

The scope of the modeling effort might be more ambitious

and require people who are competent in one or more of the following areas: statistics, programming, analysis, or operations research. As we discussed in Chapter 5 there are financial modeling languages available that do not require a technical specialist, but many organizations still use programs and approaches that necessitate a relatively sophisticated degree of support. The selection of this person, often called a liaison, is by no means an easy task.

Frequently, an individual is selected from the financial area. This person may have exhibited an interest in or flair for quantitative analysis. Given the typical background and orientation of such a person the major training effort must be devoted to increasing his understanding of financial models. This can be accomplished by attending independent seminars on the subject provided by organizations such as the American Management Associations or by attending a particular vendor's course. Most business degree programs in colleges and universities offer some type of exposure to modeling. If situations are encountered that require specialized support, the assistance of a consultant can be sought.

Consultants can be used at any stage of the modeling effort, but they are particularly useful in the early stages of analysis or to resolve well-defined technical issues that surface during the model's development. Special care must be taken to ensure that no unhealthy dependence on the external consultant develops. The consultant should not remain on the engagement too long but should train the in-house staff to do the tasks themselves. Proper use of a consultant can be an effective way to provide the specialized expertise that is sometimes required in a project. To take full advantage of this option without incurring unnecessary costs, management should make sure that the consultant doesn't perform activities that could be done more cost-effectively by in-house personnel.

Another approach to organizing the modeling effort is to

buy talent from the outside. I will differentiate two types of situations and discuss the benefits and pitfalls of each. In the first situation, the outsider is a competent model builder but does not have any direct experience in building or using financial models. The biggest drawback in this situation is that the person must not only become familiar with the nuances of the organization but also be trained in the financial area. Perhaps the greatest caveat is to avoid technically competent individuals who lack tact and are poor communicators. The net effect of selecting such people is to frustrate the modeling effort with human relations problems. By its very nature, the training process for many technical fields is devoid of exposure to the "softer" subjects such as interpersonal behavior and communications skills. This is not to say that all individuals with technical backgrounds are poor communicators. My comments are meant only to highlight a problem that has occurred in enough situations to warrant special consideration.

The second situation is perhaps more desirable. In this case an individual is hired who has both a strong technical foundation and experience in developing and implementing financial models. Where are such individuals to be found? Newly minted business school graduates rarely have the necessary experience. The obvious source is other organizations engaged in financial model development or the financial services groups of companies engaged in the marketing of financial modeling software. People of the latter group in particular, after working for a software house for a few years, often hunger for the opportunity to move into a line position that requires their expertise in financial modeling. There still remains the need to orient the individual to the organizational climate of the firm, but the technical and financial knowledge these people bring to the task can prove to be a real plus in pursuing this course of action.

Regardless of how and where the requisite personnel are

obtained, there must be a test or trial period in which the financial manager challenges the modeling group to perform useful work. This is not so obvious as it appears to be. In order to create the necessary rapport and build credibility for itself, the modeling group should be given relatively small tasks to perform. Its ability to execute its functions within resource limitations should give the financial manager an indication of its members' competence and style of working. This exercise serves several functions. First, it permits the modeling group to get to know the organization and its personnel and provides a real-world training ground. Second, it can show management that financial modeling can make a definite contribution to the organization, thereby increasing confidence in the modeling group. Finally, it limits downside risks in the event of an unsuccessful project.

Note that this approach recognizes that the effort at financial modeling must start small and increase gradually so that the organization, through its financial management, can assimilate and use the models in their decision-making framework. Grandiose models without user benefits have no place in organizations which have to produce results, whether they be profit or not-for-profit institutions.

Carefully controlled use of financial modeling can add significantly to the successful management of a company. Without proper controls, the effort can lead to needless expenditures on models that are unrealistic and frustrating to both the model builders and the financial managers.

Management Commitment and Organizational Politics

Our previous discussion has centered on the personnel issue. This by no means exhausts the range of organizational issues that must be resolved in setting up a financial modeling effort.

One of the prime factors determining the sucess or failure of the financial modeling effort is management commitment. This is a two-way street. Results contribute to commitment, and commitment creates an atmosphere that encourages results.

Management commitment must be *continuous.* Expecting too much too soon from the financial modeling activity is one of the surest ways to become disenchanted with the process of modeling. Many firms have experienced the situation in which the top "honcho" for modeling left the organization and all financial modeling activities ceased. The only logical explanation for this is that the decision makers as a group did not really believe that modeling was of any value to them. Once the pressure to use models was removed, they stopped using them. If something is perceived to be of real benefit, people do not have to be told to use it. If it really helps the financial manager come to grips with uncertainty, and if it really clarifies alternatives and is cost-effective, no coercion is needed. Certainly, top management support is a necessary condition for a successful modeling program, but it is by no means a sufficient condition.

There are other factors which have been associated with the failure of models in organizations. Our discussion will focus on politics. Politics existed in organizations before financial models came along, and it will exist as long as organizations do. To be successful, the financial modeling program must take into account the political environment of the organization and work within it. Every step of the modeling process could be, and typically is, affected by organizational political factors. Collecting data, estimating parameters, making assumptions, and generating scenario all have political implications. Tact is always necessary in dealing with people, but especially in situations that could have a direct bearing on the outcome of a modeling effort.

I will illustrate the importance of political considerations with a brief discussion of two types of model building. I will call them "modeling for justification" and "modeling for decision making."

In the case of modeling for justification, a manager has already reached a decision on which course of action to follow, and all that is needed at this time is the development of a financial model which "proves" or "legitimizes" that decision. The model builder, in this case, is instructed, either directly or indirectly, to ensure that a particular result is achieved. This approach, to say the least, takes the "art of modeling" to an extreme. The purpose of the model is to justify a previously arrived-at conclusion. The deliberate selection of an improper sample, omitting a key assumption, or failing to consider all relevant alternatives are but a few of the many ways that the results of a financial model can be "guided" to result in pre-specified outcomes. This process can hardly be called modeling, yet to an outsider the result has all the appearances of a financial model.

Modeling for decision making is what is generally regarded as modeling in the traditional sense. Here we engage in modeling to help in the process of reaching a decision and exploring different alternatives. The distinction between the two types of models raises questions of professionalism as well as ethical issues inherent in following or not following the scientific method in model development.

The reader might not fully appreciate the importance of this distinction unless he has experienced the typical political environment surrounding significant organizational decisions. A high degree of frustration is present among model builders who spend a significant portion of their time building financial models of the justification variety. On the other hand, model builders who really believe that they are contributing to the decision-making process experience a feeling of accomplishment and satisfaction. The responsibility rests with management to create a positive atmosphere in which the benefits of objective modeling are considered as a contributing factor in the decision-making process.

Is There a Best Way?

We have discussed organizational considerations in this chapter, pointing out both the benefits and limitations of different approaches to integrating the modeling effort into the organization. The obvious question is, What is the best way for me? Success and failure, as we have in seen this chapter, depend on many factors. Organization is but one. The key factor that transcends all others is trust between the model builder and the financial decision maker. The more closely the two functions are intermeshed, in my opinion, the better off the organization is going to be.

The key issue is whether it is easier to train a quantitative analyst to be a financial analyst or to train a financial analyst in the methodology of model building. My own bias is with the latter, for reasons that are based more on the person's attitude than on training in one discipline or another. I would prefer to have a person with a business or decision-making mentality responsible for the financial modeling effort. This attitude is characterized by a willingness to function in the typical decision-making arena. We typically are under time pressure and lack sufficient information to make decisions, and thus rarely know what decision is "best". Not everyone is comfortable operating in that mode. Quite often mathematicians or scientists are preoccupied with building elaborate mechanisms irrespective of time or cost considerations, have no appreciation for the time pressure of decisions, and require data that are unrealistic or unattainable.

If, after training in the methodology of modeling, there

still are weak points in the background of the financial person, as there will undoubtedly be, this can always be corrected by using outside consultants. The bottom line is that attitude is more difficult to change than are educational shortcomings. There are always exceptions to the rule, but these comments are based on my assessment of modeling efforts over the years. The ideal candidate for this type of position may be an MBA with specialization in financial management and a strong background in quantitative analysis as well as a few years experience in building and implementing financial models for organizations.

Summary

The focus of this chapter was on the organizational support structure for the financial modeling effort. We discussed the necessity to start with small projects so that a successful track record can be established within the organization.

The organizational placement of the modeling team was explored, and several options were presented. Staffing approaches were considered next. We saw that there are several different viable paths that could be followed by an organization just getting started in financial modeling. The role of outside consultants was discussed, including some advice on how to deal with a consultant. The all-important need for management concern and support for the modeling program was stressed, and issues relating to organizational politics as it affects modeling were considered.

The chapter concluded with a discussion of the ideal candidate to manage the financial modeling effort.

9

Dealing
with the Vendor

ONCE you have decided to initiate a serious effort in financial
model building there remains the critical decision as to the
approach to be taken to develop the software. There are
numerous companies offering a diverse mixture of packages.
The essential question which must be answered is, Will we
purchase a package or develop our own models?

Unfortunately, there is no easy answer to this question.
Some companies offer time-sharing—that is, they merely sell
computer time to organizations so that their financial people
are able to develop their own models and implement them on
the outside firm's computers. Other organizations, in addition
to selling computer power, make available their own version of
proprietary financial modeling software which can be used
only on their computing systems. In some cases a complete
financial modeling system is unavailable but independent

modules are provided that have the capability, when integrated, to form the nucleus of the modeling effort. For example, an extensive array of forecasting techniques might be offered along with a data base retrieval package or a file management system. Both of these modules, when augmented with financial model logic, can perform a significant number of the functions provided in many complete financial modeling systems. Obviously, significantly greater knowledge would be required of the financial manager in order to follow this approach to model building.

The time-sharing industry itself has undergone a rapid transformation over the last few years. There are several reasons for this. Many firms recognizing the potential for supporting the financial modeling efforts of organizations have evolved from simply selling time to offering a full range of support services for financial modeling—consulting, analysis, programming, and interpretation. These firms view their role as that of a member of the client's financial management team. This position is a radical shift from the early stage of the industry when time-sharing companies viewed their prime function as being merchants of convenient computing power.

The second major change agent that influenced the time-sharing industry was the potential of the minicomputer, which threatened the very existence of the industry. Today, there are several time-sharing firms that market minicomputers as well as their traditional product.

What are the implications of these developments for the firm getting started in financial model building? There are many: The typical small to medium-size firm contacts but one or two vendors and requests a presentation of their available modeling support. Notwithstanding the limitations of this approach, the vendor's philosophy on support services for the modeling effort is a critical point to be raised. If your internal modeling team is technically competent both in the modeling and financial areas, then you might not be so concerned about technical support services. On the other hand, the financial group typically finds that a significant degree of support is required especially in the early stages of the relationship.

Some of the needs that surface early are the ability to work with the proprietary modeling system and to master communicating with the vendor's control system. Often the user is given free rein to attend training sessions on either the vendor's or the user's premises. Unfortunately, the only type of training material available frequently is a poorly written, outdated user's manual and a telephone number to call if any problems arise.

The availability of support services from the vendor is one of the most significant considerations in the relationship with a software vendor. Since each firm is different in its approach and in-house talent, time-sharing vendors must be able to provide a wide range of services. The different firms providing financial modeling services have tried to target their efforts to certain types of users. Some vendors do not want to get involved in model development with the client. Their interest is in providing access to a modeling system on their computers. This type of vendor sees its principal goal as selling computer time. Its technical support staff members do not want to serve in a consulting role beyond the stage of teaching command language syntax.

On the other end of the spectrum are vendors with larger technical staffs, which seek out extensive client involvement in design specifications and model development. This type of firm usually invests more resources in training its staff and encourages a problem-solving orientation on the part of its "consultants." It is imperative that any organization thinking of doing business with a time-sharing vendor explore the vendor's attitude toward support services in the financial modeling activity.

Charges

One of the most perplexing issues in using time-shared financial modeling is the charges. Virtually all time-sharing companies utilize a billing algorithm which computes charges for the use of the various system resources. The problem arises because no two companies' billing algorithms are alike. There are unique charges for on-line storage, mounting tapes, communications, and use of the central processing unit. Charges can vary depending on priority, time of day, and billable volume. Clearly, a poorly programmed financial model could consume an extensive amount of resources and be charged accordingly. One of the most frequent complaints of financial model users is that the computing charges severely limit the flexibility they have in using the model the way they would like. Therefore, runs are curtailed, fewer alternatives are considered, and, in general, less than the full potential of the modeling effort is realized.

The best way for the potential user to determine the effect of the billing system is to have a test program loaded and run on the system and then examine the charges. There are obvious limitations on the number of times that this can be done, but it is really the only way to convert a firm's table of fees to a meaningful measure so that intelligent comparisons can be made. Past surveys of existing systems indicated a wide range of charges among the different vendors.

Usage charges and the vendor's attitude toward support are two crucial factors in selecting a particular firm. Two other equally important considerations are the existence of the appropriate financial modeling software and recommendations from existing customers. The importance of recommendations, in particular, cannot be stressed enough, because there can be great differences in the quality of support between different branch offices of the same vendor.

Quality of Vendor Technical Personnel

The nature of financial decision making is such that its influence permeates the entire organization. Modeling of financial decisions is characterized by the same degree of potential impact. What is needed for successful financial modeling is people knowledgeable in both financial and technical matters. Too often, client firms have been concerned merely with the quality level of the support specialists provided by the time-sharing firms. As we stated in Chapter 8, the ideal financial model builder is technically competent in modeling, knows the nature of financial decision making, and is an effective communicator.

During the mid-sixties and through the seventies when the interest in financial modeling was growing, many time-sharing firms found themselves ill equipped to service the varying needs of their clients. The technical representatives of the vendors were dealing with financial analysts, managers, and often controllers and simply did not have the expertise or communications skills required to perform effectively in such an environment. Communications problems developed, and eventually the vendors proceeded on a course to recruit business school graduates who could provide the support that was expected of them.

Another major factor affecting the success of the modeling effort is continuity of personnel. The very nature of the environment of the support representative encourages turnover. After a given period of time many technical representatives who have become very knowledgeable in their firm's products realize that they would prefer to apply their knowledge and skills as a member of a client's financial modeling organization. Having become somewhat familiar with the organization in their capacity as support specialists, they frequently receive offers to join as employees. The appeal of the opportunity frequently contributes to the apparently high turnover rate of vendor personnel. Since so much of successful modeling depends on the human relationships that form the basis for credibility and trust, the modeling effort could experience setbacks if too much turnover of key personnel occurs.

So far in this chapter we have focused on time-sharing vendors. Although, as a group, they make up a substantial part of the source of vendor-provided financial modeling support, they are by no means the only segment of the market. Another major supplier of financial modeling software is the system house. Such a company offers complete financial modeling support for its proprietary products. In many instances the client has the option of either using the package at the vendor's facility and pay for charges, similar to the time-sharing approach, or having the financial modeling system brought in-house and run on the client's own host systems. These packages have been made available on some minicomputer systems.

The major strategy of this group is to act as a complete storehouse of modeling expertise. Emphasis is placed on the caliber of support and consulting services. Working with an in-house team or client liaison, a system house will complete a substantial part of the development and testing of the financial model. Recently, major marketing efforts have been undertaken by these firms to increase their influence in the financial modeling arena. The degree of involvement of the support specialists from these firms can run the gamut from preliminary consulting to model development to modifications as needed.

There is an important consideration regarding the nature of the product offered by a system house. We have stated earlier in this book that the term "financial model" has received a very broad interpretation by most people. Financial modeling systems offered by firms in this category are some of the most powerful available. In addition to file management capabilities, extensive statistical routines, "conversational" financial modeling languages, and security provisions are provided. Proponents of these modeling systems maintain that only systems with these capabilities are truly modeling systems and that most other systems are only report generators. The fact of the matter is that there is no precise, generally accepted definition of financial model but rather a continuum. The financial manager must cut through the marketing semantics to analyze the functions of any proposed system.

Major accounting firms are a third major source of financial modeling systems. This activity was a natural extension of their management services activity. The major advantage that these firms possess is their familiarity with the financial activities of their clients. Either as recommendations in a management letter or otherwise, the need for better planning and control of the enterprise might be brought home to the client. To some people's thinking a natural place to seek assistance is from their accounting firm.

Most of the major accounting firms have accelerated their involvement in the modeling business by setting up special support groups geared to the various modeling needs of their clients. Since many of the people in these groups are CPAs, some financial executives are more comfortable dealing with them.

Most of the software from these firms is available in a time-sharing mode. The degree of complexity runs the gamut from isolated modules to fairly sophisticated custom-designed financial modeling software. Quite a bit of activity has taken place in the area of tax planning models, for obvious reasons.

Buy or Build Your Own?

By this time it should be clear that there are many external sources from which a firm can obtain financial modeling systems. With such a large number of alternative sources, why would a firm decide to develop its own system?

The answer most frequently given is that it will be cheaper to build your own. This might seem to be a perfectly logical response when a financial manager is presented with a vendor invoice for $50,000 for model development. At first blush the manager will be hard-pressed to tell why the cost is so high. It should be remembered that there are personnel costs and testing time on the computer, to identify just two of many cost factors. There is a hidden cost, too, that must be considered. Many commercial financial modeling systems have been designed to be as user-oriented as possible. Special consideration was given to generality of design so that many varying applications could be accommodated by the software. Typically, care was given to documentation and training materials. In many internally developed systems, corners get cut and the net effect often turns out to be a system that is incomplete, inflexible, poorly documented, and delivered at a cost substantially exceeding the original budget.

A great deal of care must be taken with the initial modeling effort. Traditionally, initial objectives—both the model developer's and the financial manager's—are too ambitious. That is why I recommended earlier to start small. After several small successes, the firm will be in a position to embark on a more ambitious project. If too much time elapses between model specification and delivery, key personnel can lose interest, which is an essential factor in maintaining executive support for the financial modeling program within a firm. In addition, if poor project control procedures are followed, the effort will tend to drift away from the original objective. Often, what results is an overly technical model which does not meet the needs or the decision-making style of the manager who originally commissioned the project. Recall my earlier comments regarding the importance of effective and continual communication between the protagonists. The financial manager would look unfavorably upon a "surprise" presented to him. If modeling is truly perceived and conducted as a process, then both parties should operate in a surprise-free environment.

After You Have Begun

Regardless of the particular approach your organization has elected to follow, there will come a time when the modeling effort is analyzed in terms of "What next?"

If you began using a time-sharing service, very soon someone will be agonizing over the skyrocketing costs of using the model. What usually happens in a successful application is that more and more applications are developed as the financial managers come to appreciate the benefits of financial modeling.

At this point, a group of people starts looking at ways to control expenses. One alternative that is usually proposed is to bring the applications inside on the department's or division's own minicomputer. This proposal can meet with several different responses. Some firms, unfortunately, discover that they are not permitted to run the financial models on their own systems. They can be used only on the vendor's system. A little bit of forward planning could avoid this situation. You are now "locked into" the vendor's system, and the costs of leaving might be greater than the costs of remaining. This can happen very easily to the first-time user of financial modeling software. As a financial manager who is just getting started in financial modeling, make sure that this does not happen to you!

Let us look at another possible reaction. Even if you are able to transfer many of the applications to your own firm, you might find that the existing data processing group vehemently objects, on the grounds of redundancy, to your proposed acquisition of a minicomputer. Although this is sometimes a valid objection, it is often more of a political response on the part of the data processing manager. I have seen some departments whose time-sharing budgets were never challenged, but once they proposed bringing in a minicomputer to reduce overall expenses, they were taken over the coals.

If a study of your financial modeling efforts does show that substantial savings would be achieved by converting to a minicomputer, then it would make sense to pursue this avenue further. This alternative is not without its potential problems, as many first-time minicomputer users have discovered the hard way. The growth of the minicomputer industry is simultaneous with the growth in the use of financial modeling. Both fields are experiencing predictable growing pains. It is one of the purposes of this book not to make you an innocent victim.

A third plausible reaction to your decision to bring your financial modeling effort in-house is to propose using your organization's existing computing resource. If the current facility is not used to full capacity, then expansion is not necessary—at least not in the short run. What typically happens is that, due to the nature of the financial modeling programs, severe degradation of the organization's computer facilities results. Friction inevitably occurs when the users of the models are asked to curtail their conversational use of the system during prime time because of the increase in the overhead that results from the use of the models. This factor has been one of the major reasons why some firms acquired a special minicomputer to support modeling or went to time-sharing in the first place.

The only way that I know of to alleviate some of the problems raised by these alternatives is to use cost/benefit analyses along with a healthy appreciation for existing corporate politics. This is why it is so essential that the members of the financial modeling team know and understand the organization in which they are a part.

Summary

In this chapter we have addressed the question of whether to purchase or develop the software for the financial modeling program. Both the pros and cons of each of several alternatives were presented. Throughout our discussion we emphasized the importance of interacting with the vendor. A final consideration was what happens to the organization once the modeling effort expands beyond its infancy and experiences its first growth pains.

10

Financial Modeling
and MIS—
The Perfect Marriage

One of the most serious mistakes that can be made by an organization just beginning a program in financial modeling is to overlook the necessity of an effective supporting information system. The emphasis of this chapter is on the organization's management information system. We will attempt to explain, in a jargon-free manner, some critical MIS concepts and the impact they can have on the creation of successful financial models.

Managerial Decisions

The principal function of information systems is to support managerial decision making by providing timely, accurate, and cost-effective information. But there is a wide spectrum of information that is needed for decision making. In this section we will discuss four of the many types of decision situations faced by management, and for each class we will discuss the interface between the financial model and the information system.

The first type of decision situation may be called structured. For many problems occurring in the daily business of running an organization, management is able to grasp the key factors that have a bearing on the decision process. The financial manager can identify the objective and the key variables, and with a little effort the functional relationships can be derived. In this case, financial modeling can serve the purpose of exploring the effects of perturbations to a base case, or it can derive an optimal solution to the model formulated by the manager. In any case, the structured problem can be attacked through financial modeling.

The opposite of the structured problem is the unstructured decision situation. This is much more difficult to model. In this situation the manager is not sure what information is needed to cope effectively with the problem at hand. The objective might be known, but the identification of the key variables and how they are related is not clear to the manager. Quite often extensive data are collected on the hunch that they might be useful. At a later stage of the modeling effort it is discovered that variables previously thought to be important were not.

Unstructured decision situations often are potentially high-payoff. The financial model builder, with his analytical orientation, can often assist the financial manager in dealing with unstructured problems. Techniques of explicit assumption making and other "quick and dirty" modeling procedures can aid the financial manager in assessing the scope and general nature of the problem at an early stage of the effort.

Even though financial modeling can be of assistance to the manager in both structured and unstructured decision situations, the ramifications are different. In the former, the information system might merely have to be accessed, whereas in the latter case, it might have to be created especially to support the decision.

The other two decision categories which we will discuss are repetitive versus one-time managerial decisions. As we will see, the two types involve conflicting information system demands.

Depending on the potential payback, it is often desirable to develop a reasonably complete information support structure for a repetitive decision. Typically, the first stage of developing this support structure concentrates on providing the information required to make a decision. Once the system is in place for some time and people become familiar with its capabilities, there is an attempt to fine-tune its performance. It is at this stage that financial modeling can be brought in to either optimize or simply improve the performance of the system. Since most models are built on the concept of balancing trade-off factors, they usually demand that new information be collected by the system. This point will be discussed later in this chapter in the section "Limitations of Accounting Systems."

Financial modeling is being employed increasingly in one-time managerial decision situations. If the stakes are high enough, management might realize that an investment in modeling might be money well spent. Examples of such high-stake one-time decisions might be new plant or warehouse acquisition, litigation strategy, or bidding for a large contract. Twenty-thousand, or even fifty-thousand, dollars spent on modeling to support a fifty-million-dollar decision is a minuscule amount if it helps management make a better decision. For the most part, I would expect the data for these types of models to be external to the firm's existing information system. It is quite possible that the data collection phase, supported by a relatively unsophisticated model, would be the largest cost component of the modeling program.

In this section, we have demonstrated how different financial models create varied demands on the information system of an organization. As a matter of fact, the presence of the model might be the change agent which stimulates a new direction to the firm's information support function.

Role of an Organization's MIS

In the first chapter of this book we classified financial modeling into three categories: strategic models, tactical models, and operational models. This three-way scheme reflects the broad categories of managerial decisions that take place in all organizations. It stands to reason that every organization must have a parallel network of information systems to support those decisions. These three types of decisions place a tremendous variety of demands on the information resources, which must provide data at various levels of detail or aggregation. The manner in which each organization services these information needs is by no means uniform. The extent of computer-based applications varies across and within industries. We can identify two general approaches that can be followed in providing information to support decisions: formal and informal systems.

Formal information systems exist because of decree. Someone in a position of responsibility decided that the particular data in the system were required to support a given level of managerial decision making. Data in these systems are collected, summarized, analyzed, and reported according to specifications developed by designers in collaboration with managers.

Informal information systems exist for an entirely different reason: they are needed, or at least thought to be needed, by the decision maker. The financial model builder must always be cognizant of the presence of informal information systems within organizations. If the model is to help decision makers make better decisions, then we should look at the information that is actually used to support decisions. Many managers, dissatisfied with the inadequacy of formal systems, have created informal information systems to help them cope with their operating environment. This is one of the major reasons why financial models often require data that are not presently available from a firm's information system.

In the next section we will look at the types of data which should be provided by an MIS.

Functional Output of an MIS

In this section we will present the general kind of information which a manager can expect from the organization's MIS. The particular role of financial modeling in the context of the information resource will also be discussed.

The backbone of any information system is the generation and use of periodic or regularly scheduled reports for management. These reports are the result of formal analyses and design activities of the systems department. A feature of many of these reports is the application of statistical analysis to help clarify trends or patterns that might be present. Statistical modeling can also be employed to reduce the sheer volume of data that is generated and must eventually be assimilated by management.

The second type of information generated by an MIS is ad hoc reports designed to provide information of particular interest to a manager. Nonperiodic in nature, they are often a by-product of a financial modeling effort. Hopefully, the results of the information provided by the report are used effectively by the manager in making decisions. Many types of forecasting studies are included in this type of reporting requirement.

The next type of output from an MIS would be some form of exception reports. Exception reports are based on coded decision rules that evaluate a large assembly of data and select exceptions, which are brought to the attention of management. Financial modeling can prove useful in this situation, because the impact of following different decision rules can be explored by the financial manager. Several strategies can be tested on past data, and a ranking can be used to determine the relative efficacy of different selection criteria. This is one of the most fruitful areas of the application of financial modeling for a company.

The last type of reporting function of an MIS is the prompt servicing of inquiries by managers. The emphasis is on satisfying immediate requests for information of a relatively uncomplicated nature. The reader should not think that just because the questions are simple, the technology necessary to handle them will also be simple. I do not believe that modeling per se makes a valuable contribution in this application. The capability required for this function is a highly flexible data management system. Creative use of data presentation—for example, graphic data display—may often be more effective in satisfying the manager's inquiries.

Limitations of Accounting Systems

Most firms have had a considerable degree of experience in collecting and using accounting data. Internal policy decisions on accounting data are supplemented and guided by proclamations from the IRS and the SEC, among others. The nature of most accounting data is historical. They are gathered to serve the reporting requirements of the firm. They lack a fundamental orientation toward the future, which is when managerial decisions will be evaluated.

The advent of model building and in particular forecasting has created a demand for information that has not been a part of the organization's traditional accounting system. Data external to the firm, for instance, are not a natural feature of an accounting system. The same can be said for many of the data that serve as input or coefficients in many financial models. An extension to a firm's accounting system must be made so that information is made available to decision makers.

There is another feature that should be discussed when considering the adequacy of accounting data for financial modeling. Although an organization might collect a vast amount of data to meet its accounting requirements, these data might be inaccessible to the model builder without extensive reformatting of fields into working files, which in itself can cause severe problems. Data that must be in a disaggregated form for the model may have been summarized for use in another application. In a situation of this type it might be easier to start from the beginning and collect the data again rather than try to recreate the required level of detail.

The incorporation of opposing cost considerations in a financial model poses an additional burden on the accounting system. Typically, the model builder has a model formulation which balances an out-of-pocket accounting-measured cost with an opportunity or intangible cost that must be determined empirically. An entire data base of information might have to be collected to support the model's data requirements. The existing accounting system is of little use to the model builder in this situation.

My comments in this section are not to be interpreted as a blanket indictment of the accounting department; rather, they express the view that an MIS must cover considerably more ground than can be normally expected of an accounting system.

The Unfulfilled Promise of MIS

MIS was one of the most famous "buzz words" of the sixties. It was promised by salesmen, academicians, and systems personnel to be the answer to all the organization's problems. Big computers supporting mammoth systems which when implemented would provide instant access by management to all the company's data—that was the promise. The reality of the situation was quite different. Systems too grandiose were envisoned by people on both sides.

When it became clear that MIS was oversold, senior management was left very skeptical about the ability of the systems staff to manage its affairs effectively. The systems function was subjected to tighter management control, and blanket requests for new systems were not approved as easily as in earlier times. Systems were expected to be cost-justified, and experimentation with various types of chargeback systems was quite common.

What was being challenged was not the concept of providing relevant, timely, and cost-effective information for management. The objection was to the all-inclusive system that would take years to develop. The concept of the total MIS gradually gave way to more tractable, if less exotic, approaches to providing for the decision makers' information needs. Functional systems were developed on the basis of modular and time-staged implementation schedules. The user, as a manager responsible for his activity, became more actively involved in the systems development effort. Expertise became more dispersed throughout the organization. This factor enabled the specifications to be kept more realistic and implementation performance monitored more closely.

It might be noted that a similar phenomenon is occurring in the modeling environment. As more users become aware of the capabilities and limitations of a technology, we can expect more realistic expectations on the part of all concerned. Originally models were sold on the basis of replacing a whole level of managers within the organization. This never happened, partly because it was quickly realized that the purpose of modeling was to support decision makers and not to supplant them. Both computers and models were marketed incorrectly to users, creating expectations that only time and experience could put into perspective. Successful users of both technologies recognize them for what they really are— powerful tools for the enlightened decision maker.

Traditional File versus Data Base

Improvements in data storage media and increasing information demands by managers have played a primary role in drawing attention to limitations of traditional file processing concepts. In the past, each new data processing application developed for a company required one or more new data files. As programs proliferated, so did data files. The nature of most applications was such that there was a high degree of overlap among the data items in the files. Aside from increased data storage costs, a more significant side effect occurred: the number and size of the files made it virtually impossible to update all files with similar information at reasonable intervals. The net result was that there were several versions of the same data field simultaneously in existence within the organization. This situation caused, and still causes, enormous difficulties for decision makers, who may find themselves using incorrect data in deriving forecasts and estimating critical parameter values. There is no way to cross-check every data item without incurring enormous costs and time delays. An excellent model could be giving erroneous results because of the poor data on which it is based.

The recognition of this untenable situation led to the concept of a data base. Although the supporting software can get very complex, the basic concept of the data base is quite simple to grasp. Instead of a proliferation of physically distinct files, there is one physical file capable of being logically segmented to support the data requirements of several application programs. Essential data are entered but once by the originating unit and are available for use by all other authorized applications. The redundancy of the traditional file concept is minimized, and there are greater safeguards to maintain the integrity of the data.

The financial model builder is one step closer to data that have a high degree of credibility. There are typically more extensive data edit checks in a data base environment, since the often conflicting requirements of many users movquacust be satisfied. Once the key variables for a given modeling application have been identified and security clearance has been received, the model builder can create a logical file of the specified data fields.

There is one additional comment regarding the use of data bases by the model builder. Most of the data in the data base will be current data, since most information systems require this kind of data. There may be some conflict when the financial model builder needs historical data in order to use certain forecasting and parameter estimation techniques. We only mention this fact so that some provision can be made for financial model builders who find themselves in a data base environment.

Security of Data Files

When each application had its own data file, users felt more secure about the preservation of the integrity of their data. The advent of a data base environment predicated on the concept of data sharing has caused managers to become more concerned about the security precautions taken by the systems group for the data. Most data base systems offer a multilevel security capability. Security control can be at the data base, file, or data item level. In addition, specific controls can be placed on programs.

These security features guarantee that access can be controlled and limited to those functions or people who have a valid right to the data. Once managers are convinced of the safeguards built into the system, there will be a greater willingness to cooperate in the data base project. There will always be political and territorial issues, however, that cannot be avoided. For example, the production manager might be concerned that his information will be misused by the marketing group.

The financial model builder who uses the company's data base will be treated no differently from anyone else. There must be a valid "need to know" before he is authorized to access specific data fields. If a need arises for more data during the course of the financial model-building effort, then there must be an additional evaluation before the data are released for analysis. In this way, all managers are assured of the existence of and adherence to procedures protecting the integrity of the data base. Financial model builders, as a general rule, will find that operating in a data base environment gives them access to useful data stored at a more disaggregated level than was the case previously. This situation is because data captured at a detailed level can be aggregated by computer routines to the desired level of summary as dictated by the application. The computational burden is placed on the computer and not on people.

In conclusion, the evolution of data base development should be carefully watched by the financial model builder. Most sophisticated financial modeling systems have the capabilities of data base interface and security controls.

Distributed Data Processing—What to Expect

Distributed data processing (DDP) is another factor that will have a profound effect on the life of the financial model builder. During the past several years organizations have experienced the beginning of a trend toward increased use of the minicomputer. As more and more minicomputers were installed, it soon became evident that a larger share of information processing could be borne by the users operating at their remote locations. Instead of shipping all input to central locations for processing, organizations began to analyze the nature of their data processing work more closely. What many firms discovered was that a great deal of processing could be performed locally and required relatively little communication with the central site. Minis were installed at remote locations (departments, divisions, plants) with telecommunications capability to the central computer if data sharing was required.

Users liked the increased responsiveness of this arrangement, because it appeared to satisfy their system development needs more effectively. The trend toward greater miniaturization, along with increased computing power, portends an even greater shift in this direction in the future.

What will be the impact of DDP on financial modeling? There will be several obvious trends. First, many users will off-load their time-sharing applications to in-house minicomputers, especially if their only need for time-sharing is raw computing power and not special languages or data bases. Second, model building efforts will be brought closer to the user in the remote location. Individual departments will be able to justify minicomputers for a given application. Excess time on the machine will encourage new applications directed at helping the decision maker cope with real problems. Model development time can be reduced thanks to reduced organizational bureaucracy, and more use can be made of "quick and dirty" but effective procedures. Third, the development of application programs in one department could be easily transferred to other compatible systems in the organization. This diffusion will keep development costs for routine or repetitive applications under control.

A final, yet significant benefit of DDP would be its impact on decision making. Distributed processing puts a computer virtually at the disposal of the decision maker. As managers become more familiar with the power of the computer to support their decision-making responsibilities, they can be expected to adopt the tool as an essential element of their overall approach to making decisions. At the present time, most of us perceive the computer as a monolithic machine which can print a large amount of checks or invoices, not as a viable component of our tool kit. I strongly believe that it is just a matter of time before the combined impact of the minicomputer and financial modeling will be felt across a wider audience of organizations. The technology is already here; we are just learning how to use it effectively.

Interface between the Model Builder and the Systems Designer

So far in this chapter we have discussed aspects of management information systems that have or will have a profound impact on financial model building. There is, in reality, no practical way to separate the two. This fact is recognized by many firms that have a centralized modeling group. This group often reports to a vice president for information systems.

The reader should not conclude that the systems group does the same thing as the financial model builder. The systems designer is responsible for the development of information systems that support managerial decision making. These systems often incorporate a financial model as an essential element. Both functions exist to support and improve the quality of managerial decision making. The systems person usually has a better technical understanding of the hardware and software of an organization. The financial model builder usually has a better understanding of quantitative analysis. They both should have a thorough knowledge of the financial aspects of the organization. Financial models should be embedded in the information systems of the company. They should not exist apart from the information system. If they do, then they will not be used by the financial manager.

The financial model builder must recognize and appreciate the interpersonal dynamics of organizations. Ignorance of these factors in the early stages of developing an intiative in financial modeling can lead to costly if not irreparable damage to the entire modeling program.

Summary

In this chapter we have focused on the natural relationship between financial modeling and the organization's management information system. After discussing the nature of managerial decision making, we looked at the role of an organization's MIS. Attention was directed to the various kinds of output that an information system should produce. We saw that a firm's accounting system, in and of itself, is not sufficient to be called an MIS. An MIS, we held, is something far more extensive than the collection and reporting of financial data. Some of the reasons why the concept of MIS has been much maligned were examined.

The importance of the trend toward a data base environment was discussed as it related to the traditional file concept. Two other important topics—data security and distributed data processing—were considered next, and their eventual impact on the financial modeling effort was assessed. Finally, the interface between the systems designer and the financial model builder was discussed.

Annotated List
of References

I have included a list of books and articles which will help the reader extend his understanding of financial model building. For each major topic in the book I have assembled a collection of readings which typically delve into the subject to a greater degree than possible in a book of this nature. Rather than a mere list, I have given either an overview of the contents or a presentation of the author's conclusion. It is hoped that the interested reader will find this helpful in getting started in financial modeling.

What Is Modeling?

John S. Hammond III, "Do's and Don'ts of Computer Models for Planning," *Harvard Business Review*, March–April 1974, pp. 110–123.

The author presents a ten-stage plan for the development of a model. A section is devoted to a discussion of the organizational climate which envelops the modeling program. The most significant part of the article enumerates many of the factors within the manager's control. The author demonstrates a fine understanding of the real situation. The final section of the article presents an illustrative example which highlights the art as well as the science of model building.

Robert H. Hayes and Richard L. Nolan, "What Kind of Corporate Modeling Functions Best?" *Harvard Business Review*, May–June 1974, pp. 102–112.

The authors survey the major approaches to corporate modeling— bottom-up, top-down, and inside-out. After a lengthy discussion of the pros and cons of each approach they conclude that the inside-out approach is the most promising. Models, they point out, should be judged by their usefulness and adequacy rather than by their realism. Page 103 contains a very informative table which provides a good summary of the major ideas expressed in the article.

Thomas H. Naylor and M. James Mansfield, "The Design of Computer-Based Planning and Modeling Systems," *Long Range Planning*, February 1977, pp. 16–25.

The authors describe what they believe are the eight components that must constitute any planning and modeling system. The eight elements are: a planning system, a management information system, a modeling system, a forecasting system, econometric modeling capability, user orientation of the system, system availability, and lastly a software system. The entire article is an elaboration of these eight items, The last section of the article can serve as a preliminary checklist for features of a planning and modeling system.

Thomas H. Naylor, *Corporate Planning Models*, Reading, Massachusetts: Addison-Wesley, 1979.

This is an important book written by one of the principal architects of SIMPLAN, a powerful financial modeling language. All types of models are discussed. For example, there are chapters on marketing and production models as well as financial planning models. Naylor and his coauthors present five extensive case studies of corporate planning models in use today. The reader might also find the appendix on SIMPLAN of special interest. This is a must book for anyone interested in corporate planning models.

Patrick Rivett, *Principles of Model Building*, New York: Wiley and Sons, 1972.

In this book, Rivett explores the range of models and their applications to business organizations. The focus of the book is on problems and what might be appropriate solution procedures. The author's style is eminently readable, and the reader should find his coverage of accounting data and organizational objectives of particular interest.

Albert N. Schrieber, ed., *Corporate Simulation Models*, Seattle: University of Washington, 1970.

This is a classic book on the subject of corporate models. Although somewhat dated, it is a compendium of 25 papers that can still be of use to the model builder. The majority of the papers present attempts at modeling in various organizations. From these expositions the reader can learn a great deal about the problems which will be encountered as he enters the field of financial model building.

Surveys of Corporate Model Use

Ephraim R. McLean, "A Chief Executive Perspective on Computer-Based Planning," UCLA Working Paper, December 1977.

The author conducted a mail survey among the CEOs of 1,240 industrial, financial, and other organizations as to their corporate planning practices and the extent of their use of computer-based planning models. Responses were received from 410 firms, with 321 CEOs responding personally. The majority of firms reported that they have a five-year planning horizon, prepare these plans annually, make use of a corporate planning department, and employ a number of different planning tools and techniques. In 60 percent of the firms surveyed, computer-based planning models are used, and the overall attitude of CEOs toward this technique is quite favorable.

Richard H. McClure and Robert E. Miller, "The Application of Operations Research in Commercial Banking Companies," *Interfaces*, February 1979, pp. 24–29. (*Interfaces* is an application-oriented publication of the Institute of Management Science.)

This paper presents a snapshot view of the current level of use of operations research by 52 of the 100 largest commercial banking companies in the United States. The paper indicates which operations research methods are being used for a selected set of 18 important problems in commercial banking, a measure of the extent that various operations research methods are used for specified problems, and in what ways bank size affects the use of operations research by the banks. Forecasting and simulation led the list.

Thomas H. Naylor and Horst Schauland, "A Survey of Users of Corporate Planning Models," *Management Science*, May 1976, pp. 927–937.

This article reports on a survey of 346 companies responding to a questionnaire aimed at answering the following questions:

Who is using corporate models?
Why are they being used?
How are they used?
Which resources are required?
Which techniques and structures are employed?
What are the costs and benefits?
What enhancements are planned?
What is the future of corporate modeling?

Forecasting Models

Spyros Makridakis and Steven C. Wheelwright, *Interactive Forecasting*, 2nd Edition, San Francisco: Holden-Day. 1978.

The authors present a comprehensive analysis of many forecasting techniques. The emphasis of the book is on an interactive forecasting system known as SIBYL/RUNNER. Complete descriptions of more than 20 techniques are provided. One of the significant contributions of this book is that it provides a large variety of cases for interactive forecasting, including many of a financial nature. These cases are clearly identified as to the intended area of application. A valuable compendium of techniques and a must for the library of anyone interested in forecasting and model building.

N. Carroll Mohn and John C. Reid, "Some Practical Guidelines for the Corporate Forecaster," *Interfaces*, May 1977, pp. 70–75.

The authors summarize in this article the results obtained from a conference on major issues in the implementation of forecasts. Topics covered range from the use of probabilistic measures to the most effective means of communicating the results of forecasts. There is a particularly interesting table presented on page 73 which identifies the advantages and disadvantages of using simple and complex forecasting techniques. A final discusssion is devoted to representative "horror stories" from the corporate forecasting environment.

Steven C. Wheelwright and Spyros Makridakis, *Forecasting Methods for Management*, New York: Wiley and Sons, 1973.

This book presents an excellent nontechnical discussion of the major techniques of forecasting. Plenty of actual examples of the techniques are included along with a discussion on the interpretation of model results. One of the major contributions of the book, in my opinion, is the chapter on organizing and implementing a corporate forecasting function. Very little technical background is required to understand the concepts.

Optimization Models

J. Wesley Barnes and Robert M. Crisp, Jr., "Linear Programming: A Survey of General-Purpose Algorithms," *AIIE Transactions*, September 1975, pp. 212–221.

This article contains an excellent review of the major approaches to solving linear programming problems. The predominantly verbal description provides a concise yet thorough overview of the work in the field. An interesting section deals with some of the features of commercial codes. An itemization of references by algorithm type might prove to be helpful to the interested reader.

Frank J. Fabozzi and Joseph Valente, "Mathematical Programming in American Companies: A Sample Survey," *Interfaces*, November 1976, pp. 93–98. According to the authors, the purpose of the survey was to derive answers to the following four questions: (1) Who is adopting mathematical programming models? (2) What has been the quality of the results? (3) In which specific areas have such models been used? (4) Why have some firms not adopted mathematical programming techniques? A questionnaire was mailed to 1,000 firms in 1974. Results are based on 184 responses.

George C. Philippatos, *Financial Management Theory and Techniques,* San Francisco: Holden-Day, 1973.

This is a survey textbook on financial management. It is included in the reference list to enable the reader to obtain a detailed explanation of many of the quantitative techniques presented in our book. Particular attention is directed to the sections on mathematical programming procedures and simulation modeling. Some mathematical background is expected of the reader.

Simulation Modeling

Irwin Kabus, "You Can Bank on Uncertainty," *Harvard Business Review,* May–June 1976, pp. 95–105.

The author presents a technique which is being used by the financial modeling group at Morgan Guaranty Trust. It is called histogramming and is an attempt to capture the degree of certainty of an individual's expectations about the outcome of some future event. The concept is an excellent extension of the ideas which we presented in the chapters on simulation. The author uses an example from the financial decision-making area of a bank. The article emphasizes the importance of capturing the true expectations of the decision maker.

Dale W. Merriam and Joseph W. Wilkinson, "Model for Planning and Feedforward Control," *Managerial Planning,* March–April 1977, pp. 31–40.

The authors present a simulation model which generates an income statement to support an organization's planning function. Their model is probabilistic in nature, and the authors explain the procedure used to derive the estimates that serve as key input variables for the model. A test of the model in a small manufacturing firm is also described.

Richard C. Murphy, "A Computer Model Approach to Budgeting," *Management Accounting,* June 1975, pp. 34–38.

The author indicates that budgeting models can be broken down into three major components: (1) a report description outlining the line-by-line format of the desired output, typically following the format of a P&L statement; (2) a structure of algebraic logic or procedures underlying the computations required in the budgeting using simple formulas; (3) elements of data which, when passed through the computational processes, will generate the desired report. An interesting feature of this article is the presentation of an outline of a consolidated budget model.

John Wagner and LeRoy J. Pryor, "Simulation and the Budget: An Integrated Model," *Sloan Management Review*, Winter 1971, pp. 45–58.

The authors present an excellent exposition of the use of simulation in the budgeting process. A case example illustrates the development of a financial model. Several scenarios are explored and the results presented. This article is useful for the novice financial model builder who wants to get acquainted with a simple simulation model.

Sensitivity Analysis in Modeling

Robert W. Blanning, "The Sources and Uses of Sensitivity Information," *Interfaces*, August 1974, pp. 32–38.

Blanning presents a four-part classification system for obtaining sensitivity data from models. The four approaches are analytical calculations, repetition, post-optimal analysis, and transformation. I find the most significant contribution of this article to be the author's postulation of a metamodel which serves as the guiding vehicle for the performance of sensitivity analyses. It is an intriguing concept even with the limitations identified by the author.

Jerry W. Durway, "Sensitivity Analysis and Simulation," *Infosystems*, May 1979, pp. 70–76.

The emphasis of this article is on the use of probabilistic simulation models combined with the power of sensitivity analysis. The author demonstrates the flexibility of interactive financial modeling. The principal vehicle for the author's presentation is an interactive financial model which was developed using one of the many financial modeling packages available to the model builder. The output generated reflects a deterministic model. The model is then augmented to include probabilistic features. A comparison of the results proves very informative.

Donald A. Krueger and John M. Kohlmeier, "Financial Modeling and 'What If' Budgeting," *Management Accounting*, May 1972, pp.25–30.

This is an informative and clear exposition of the concept and power of "what if" modeling. Since the focus is on budgeting, the reader should easily grasp the potential benefits of the approach. The authors identify common problems encountered in a budgeting application and show how "what if" models can be of assistance. The authors stress the power of the approach, especially its ability to rapidly generate a number of alternatives.

J. Ravin and M. Schatzoff, "An Interactive Graphics System for Analysis of Business Decisions," *IBM Systems Journal,* June 1973, pp. 238–256.

The authors describe a graphics system which can be used to enhance the man–machine dialog during the model-building process. Although the book is somewhat dated, the reader can still appreciate its benefits while contemplating the impact of adding a graphics capability to a financial model. The reader is taken step by step through an exercise of model building with a graphics terminal.

Financial Data Banks

Joel W. Darrow, "Financial Data Banks: A Guide for the Perplexed," *Computer Decisions,* January 1975, pp. 47–54.

The author presents an interesting list of financial data banks that are available for use by the model builder. A running commentary on the features of some of the data bases is included for the benefit of the reader. Quite often a company must supplement its internal data base with external environmental data. Sometimes the only economical way to obtain these data is to subscribe to a data base through a service bureau. This and the next reference are excellent starting points to help the reader think about the revelant issues.

Joel W. Darrow, "Harnessing Other People's Data Banks," *Interfaces,* August 1975, pp. 58–65.

This article should be read with its companion from *Computer Decisions.* In this article the author provides the reader with a pair of checklists for use in selecting an external data base from a vendor. The first checklist is for the specific application for which the data are needed. The second list can be used to evaluate a particular data bank. The author divides readily available financial data into three classes:

security market data, corporation data, and economic time series. The article contains much valuable data unlikely to be outdated in the foreseeable furture.

Financial Modeling Packages

Association of Computer Users
P.O. Box 9003
Boulder, Colorado 80301

This organization publishes a directory of reports which would be of interest to the organization just getting started in financial model building. I will single out three of these reports:

- ° *Financial Modeling Languages* — This report lists the names, addresses, and other pertinent data on firms that market financial modeling software.
- ° *Interactive Data Base Systems* — The same type of vendor information is supplied, but the focus is on interactive data base systems.
- ° *Interactive Statistical Packages* — This report supplies vendor and products information on many of the routines which will form the basis for an organization's financial forecasting systems.

Real Decisions Corporation
870 High Ridge Road
Stamford, Connecticut

This company has developed a series of six standardized benchmark applications which are coded and run on systems to determine information on the following factors: relative cost, ease of use, completeness, documentation, storage and connect charges, and special analyses. A report was issued under the title *Financial Modeling Decisions*. This report is a storehouse of useful information on the various systems available. Many vendors have copies which can be reviewed by the potential model builder.

Implementation Considerations

Herbert Halbrecht et al., "Through a Glass Darkly," *Interfaces,* August 1972, pp. 1–17.

This article is a summary of a discussion by five panel members who addressed the issues of the relationship between modeler and manager, implementation guidelines, and the impact of model building on the organization. The authors are from a variety of organizations and represent a multiplicity of perspectives. Although the article was published in 1972, it is just as true today as it was when it was originally written. We still haven't learned!

Henry C. Lucas, Jr., *The Implementation of Computer-Based Models*, New York: National Association of Accountants, 1976.

To quote the author's preface, "this monograph presents the results of a study of the implementation of interactive computer models. The successful implementation of such models has been rare in actual practice, and there is increasing interest. . . . in learning more about implementation." Rather than looking at technical issues, Lucas concentrates on behavior barriers to the implementation of models in organizations.

Thomas H. Naylor, "The Politics of Corporate Model Building," *Planning Review*, January 1975.

The views of Naylor on corporate modeling are always of interest, and this article is no exception. He presents the opinion that, as a group, model builders are not good politicians. In this article the author tries to illuminate the various types of political battles that can take place in and around the corporate modeling effort. Naylor concludes his discussion with a series of do's and don'ts for the corporate model builder.

Martin K. Starr, "The Politics of Management Science," *Interfaces*, Vol. 1, 4:31–37.

The author is the editor-in-chief of *Management Science*, which is one of the most prestigious journals on applied modeling. His views on the subject are worth reading. Of particular interest is his classification system for modeling success based on the degree of understanding between the manager and the model builder. The author also presents a useful discussion of the manager and the model builder in the context of transactional analysis.

MIS and Model Building

Gerald M. Hoffman, "The Contribution of Management Science to Management Information," *Interfaces*, November 1978, pp. 34–39.

The author presents his view that the management scientist structures unstructured problems while the systems analyst exploits the inherent structure of a problem in order to incorporate that structure into a system which will yield usable and consistent results. Using several examples from his personal experience, the author makes a strong argument in favor of his position.

Raymond McLeod, Jr., *Management Information Systems*, Chicago: Science Research Associates, 1979.

This is an introductory textbook on management information systems. The reader will find the sections dealing with functional information requirements quite useful. These systems are for financial, marketing, and manufacturing information. Chapter 9 on computer support for problem solving gives a brief overview of how models can be part of an organization's information system.

Index

140

F